THE PRIESTHOOD OF ALL BELIEVERS IN THE TWENTY-FIRST CENTURY

The Priesthood of All Believers in the Twenty-First Century

*Living Faithfully as the Whole People of God
in a Postmodern Context*

∽

ROBERT A. MUTHIAH

PICKWICK *Publications* · Eugene, Oregon

Pickwick Publications
A Division of Wipf and Stock Publishers
199 W. 8th Ave., Suite 3
Eugene, OR 97401

www.wipfandstock.com

ISBN 13: 978-1-60608-094-8

Cataloging-in-Publication data:

Muthiah, Robert A.

The priesthood of all believers in the twenty-first century : living faithfully as the whole people of God in a postmodern context / Robert A. Muthiah.

viii + 186 p. ; 23 cm. — Includes bibliographical references.

ISBN 13: 978-1-60608-094-8

1. Priesthood, Universal. 2. Postmodernism—Religious aspects. 3. Theology, Practical. 4. Christian communities. I. Title.

BV4525 M95 2009

Manufactured in the U.S.A.

Contents

Acknowledgments

First and foremost, I want to thank my wife, Lisa, for walking with me as I worked on this project. Her words of support and affirmation sustained me throughout the process. Indirectly, our three children, Samuel, Isabelle, and Ezra, have also encouraged me as they point me to life outside my academic world.

I am deeply indebted to my two academic mentors, Dr. Mark Lau Branson and Dr. Veli-Matti Kärkkäinen. Their guidance, insight, and encouragement have significantly shaped the ways I do theology and their influence is present throughout this project.

Our community at Pasadena Mennonite Church has been crucial for me during this process. This community has nurtured me in the faith and has helped me to keep connecting my focused theological work to broader gospel issues of love, hope, death, life, peace, and justice.

Introduction

CONTOURS OF THE PROJECT

The priesthood of all believers is part of the ecclesiality of the church and yet current theologies, church structures, and practices often work *against* the development of congregations that involve the whole people of God in ministry. While Luther lifted up the priesthood of all believers as a key aspect of the church, in the centuries since then the importance assigned to this theology has ebbed and flowed. There is never a time, however, when the priesthood of all believers is *not* crucial in the life of the church—it belongs to the *esse*, not the *bene esse*, of the church.

This project argues for a fresh understanding and embodiment of the priesthood of all believers. Championing the priesthood of all believers has been a mark of renewal movements in the church for centuries and such voices have been heard throughout the whole range of theological traditions, especially since the 1960s. The originality of this work lies in the construction of an argument that puts a trinitarian ecclesiology, postmodern culture, and congregational practices in dialogue.

To set the framework for the discussion, we will examine the New Testament's relationship to the priesthood of all believers and get an overview the contemporary theological discussions around this topic (ch. 2). Specific texts as well as overarching themes in Scripture are explored in order to show how this theology took shape in the NT churches. The contemporary discussion is introduced by touching on several historical turning points related to the royal priesthood. We examine contemporary ecumenical perspectives by analyzing relevant Vatican II and World Council of Churches documents before turning to perspectives from within the Free Church tradition (my own location). A number of Free Church voices are highlighted with deeper analysis given to the contributions of John Howard Yoder and Miroslav Volf. This chapter points to the diversity of views regarding the content of the theology of the priesthood of all believers and foreshadows the ecclesiology that will be developed in the next chapter.

The theology of the priesthood of all believers promoted in this project is grounded through an examination of the correspondence between the Trinity and church (ch. 3). We will see how this correspondence is evident in the charisms that shape the church. A pneumatological ecclesiology emerges from this examination of the Trinity and the charisms, an ecclesiology that points to the priesthood of all believers as a social entity that is egalitarian, non-dominating, unified, and differentiated. After this view of the royal priesthood is developed, we will look at its implications for ordination, a place where one's true understanding of the church is revealed.

This ecclesiology must be lived out in the context of postmodernity, which provides both opportunities and obstacles for the church to live as the priesthood of all believers. The church always exists in the context of other social institutions, but the church must never simply adopt the values of those institutions. To explore the relationship between postmodernity and the royal priesthood, we will look at how three overarching institutions of postmodernity—globalization, individualism, and *technique*—relate to an understanding and embodiment of the priesthood of all believers (ch. 4). The church must be critically aware of its cultural context if the church is to live as the priesthood of all believers in the midst of competing structural and moral alternatives without compromising its identity.

My interest here is in doing practical theology, and therefore I work to make explicit connections between these ecclesiological and cultural discussions and the life of the local church. While such connections are made throughout, this is done in an extended way by looking at social practices (ch. 5) to show how a theology of the priesthood of all believers both contributes to and emerges from congregational praxis. We will discuss and add to Alasdair MacIntyre's conception of social practices in order to speak of *Christian* practices. Five exemplary congregational practices emerge and find connection to the priesthood of all believers. For these practices to flourish interpretive leadership is needed in our congregations, thus, we consider the nature of the interpretive task and call attention to the way it contributes to the vibrancy of congregational practices that embody and inform a theology of the priesthood of all believers. The final chapter (ch. 6) raises issues for further research and discussion.

METHOD

Because this is a work in practical theology, an explanation of methodology is important. Friedrich Schleiermacher is commonly viewed as the father of practical theology. In his *Brief Outline on the Study of Theology* he divided the study of theology into three parts: philosophical theology, historical theology, and practical theology.[1] The development of practical theology as an academic discipline grew out of Schleiermacher's schema. Although Schleiermacher's approach initially may appear to give an equal valuing to these three parts, Schleiermacher actually viewed practical theology as secondary to philosophical and historical theology. Although he referred to practical theology as "the crown of theological studies,"[2] he in fact treated practical theology as the *servant* of theological studies. In his view, the purpose of practical theology was to simply implement what had been determined by philosophical and historical theology. In speaking about the actions of practical theology, Schleiermacher said:

> It is not among the aims of practical theology to teach the right conception of these tasks. Rather, presupposing this, it has only to do with correct procedures for executing all the tasks which are to be included within the notion of 'Church leadership.'[3]

The role of practical theology for Schleiermacher was that of applying theory to practice.

In contrast, I view practical theology as the reflection upon the *mutually informing* nature of concepts and actions. Our actions themselves are theory laden and thus they *embody* theology rather than just *apply* theology. All our actions have theological content; the task of practical

1. Schleiermacher, *Brief Outline on the Study of Theology*.
2. Ibid., 125.
3. Ibid., 92.

theology is to bring this content to the surface for articulation, reflection, and modification. This project builds on the assumption that theology shapes actions and actions shape theology.

Another undergirding assumption is that the Holy Spirit is present and at work as the community moves back and forth between reflection and action, so practical theology is more than an exercise in social science. The Spirit brings the presence of Christ to the process through the word, church tradition, and the living community. So I understand practical theology to be a pneumatological endeavor.

We employ a critical correlational approach to practical theology, similar to that set forth by Don Browning.[4] Correlations are made between the Trinity, Scripture, and the church, as well as between the stated theology of the church and the church's practices. This approach is called critical because it evaluates these correlations.

Browning's model of practical theology includes four movements: descriptive theology, historical theology, systematic theology, and strategic practical theology.[5] Because Browning sees action as integrally related with understanding and interpretation, Browning's fourth movement, strategic practical theology, is not merely the application of theory to practice. Like the other movements, this movement, too, is reflective. In addition, this fourth movement is present in the other three movements; questions of action interpenetrate the theoretical movements all along.[6]

Accordingly, this project begins with application in mind. Questions regarding the nature of the priesthood of all believers arose out of my congregational experience, and so behind the theological and cultural sections (historical, systematic, and descriptive theology) always lurks the question of how this discussion relates to the local church (strategic practical theology). The arguments in ch. 5 on Christian practices make explicit the intertwined nature of theory and practice and drive for a re-integration of the conversation into the life of the local church.

Several terms are used interchangeably to refer to the idea that all Christians share in the ministry of the church. The "priesthood of all believers," a phrase used by Martin Luther, is one of these. The "royal priesthood," a phrase found in 1 Peter 2:9, is another. At points I use "the

4. Browning's approach, in turn, follows closely that of David Tracy. Browning, *A Fundamental Practical Theology*, 44.

5. Ibid., 8 and passim.

6. Ibid., 57.

common priesthood," a phrase often used in Catholic circles where the phrase "the priesthood of all believers" is avoided because of its association with Luther and the Reformation. Other phrases used as synonyms include "the universal priesthood" and "the whole people of God." This general idea will be given more specific content as we go.

TWO

New Testament and Theological Perspectives on the Priesthood of All Believers

The priesthood of all believers is a key idea Luther addressed. His work brought to the church a new perspective. We must be aware, however, that this idea goes back much further than Luther, and the discussions of his day brought no finality to the debate regarding the content and praxis of this idea—the debate remains lively today.

As we seek to understand what the priesthood of all believers might mean for us today, we must be cognizant of the fact that we are not starting from scratch. We have rich material from both the Scriptures and the history of the church to draw upon. It will be my goal in this chapter to draw on these rich traditions in order to set the framework for the ensuing discussion. In the first section, I explore words, patterns, and themes in the NT that relate to the priesthood of all believers. In the second section, I pick up the theological discussions of this doctrine. After pointing to key historical turning points, I will focus on the discussion from the 1960s to the present. The second section will conclude by looking specifically at how the Free Church theologians, John Howard Yoder and Miroslav Volf, handle the idea of the priesthood of all believers. In this way I will lay the foundation for the critical and constructive work to follow.

NEW TESTAMENT ISSUES

The most obvious place to start, when exploring the doctrine of the priesthood of all believers in the New Testament, is with the texts that appear to speak most explicitly of a universal priesthood. A second approach is to look for patterns or themes that emerge from the Scriptures.[1]

The Historically Key Passage: 1 Peter 2:4–10

Four NT passages explicitly apply priesthood language to Christians (1 Pet 2:4–10; Rev 1:6; 5:10; and 20:6). The passage that has traditionally been most closely connected to the priesthood of all believers is 1 Peter 2:4–10, especially vv. 5 and 9.[2] The scholarly consensus is that the audience was primarily Gentile.[3] Peter's intention seems to be to get the Gentiles to embrace the scriptures, stories, and the Messiah of Judaism.[4]

Peter promotes the authority of the Jewish Scriptures by citing them frequently in his letter. Paul Achtemeier notes that a distinctive of this passage is that it contains one of the most concentrated sets of OT citations to be found in the entire NT.[5] Of particular interest for our discussion are the Jewish scriptures Peter chose to cite. Of the hundreds of OT references to priests and the priesthood, Peter selected only from the few that refer to the *whole* people in priestly terms.[6] The background to the "holy priesthood" of v. 5 and the "holy nation" of v. 9 is Exod 19:6 where God gives the following words to Moses to pass on to the people: "you shall

1. Richard B. Hays argues that we should undertake the hermeneutical task by appealing to scripture in four different ways: we should look for rules, principles, paradigms, and symbolic worlds. Rules are "direct commandments or prohibitions of specific behavior." Principles are "general frameworks of moral consideration by which particular decisions about action are to be governed." Paradigms are "stories or summary accounts of characters who model exemplary conduct." A symbolic world "creates the perceptual categories through which we interpret reality." Hays, *The Moral Vision of the New Testament*, 208, 209. We do not really have any rules in scripture regarding church structure and the priesthood of all believers. Hays's second and third modes of appeal, however, *are* helpful to us as we look to scripture for insight. We will get to his fourth mode, symbolic worlds, when we look at John Howard Yoder below.

2. The passages from Revelation read as follows: "and made us to be a kingdom, priests serving his God and Father" (1:6); "you have made them to be a kingdom and priests serving our God" (5:10); and "they will be priests of God and of Christ" (20:6). All refer to the whole body of believers, not to a priestly class within that body. (All scripture quotations are from the NRSV.)

3. Michaels, *1 Peter*, 7; Achtemeier, *1 Peter*, 51.; Hillyer, *1 and 2 Peter, Jude*, 4.

4. Michaels, *1 Peter*, 8–10.

5. Achtemeier, *1 Peter*, 150.

6. Robinson, "Christianity's 'No' to Priesthood," 12; cf. Elliott, "Elders as Leaders in 1 Peter and the Early Church."

be for me a priestly kingdom and a holy nation" (the "royal priesthood" in v. 9 is a quotation from the LXX rendering of Exod 19:6).[7] Alluding to Isa 43:20–21, which refers to the whole people of Israel, not to a chosen class within that nation, v. 9 goes on to speak of a "chosen people," who is to proclaim God's mighty acts. Peter's grounding of his conception of the royal priesthood in these carefully selected OT texts shows his theology of a royal priesthood to consciously include the whole people of God.

New Testament scholars call into question the notion that these verses mean each person can interpret Scripture for him/herself because each person is a priest. One problem with this understanding is that 1 Pet 2: 5, 9; Exod 19:6; and Isa 43:20–21 all refer to a corporate entity. None of these references describe individuals as priests. It is the entire nation, the chosen people, who constitute the priesthood in these passages. Thus, an individualistic understanding does not find textual support. A second problem has to do with the idea that this passage refers to the function of interpreting Scripture. This problem must be set in the context of a larger debate about whether this passage, in talking about priesthood, is referring to a status or a function.

John Elliot argues that priesthood in 1 Pet 2 refers to the status of believers. He is a strong advocate for the view that the focus of these verses is on election, arguing that Peter wants these congregations to view themselves as God's elect in the same way as the people of Israel were God's elect.[8] This would be consistent with the letter's purpose of grounding the readers in the history of Israel. Elliot argues that the author is not pointing to the functional nature of the priesthood and so he holds that this passage says nothing about church authority or structure. Raymond Brown also eschews a functional interpretation, but rather than election, he holds that the focus here is on priestly holiness.[9] Believers are to be marked by the holiness that was associated with the priesthood in the OT. Everett Ferguson points out that the priesthood of all believers came to mean that individuals can approach God without a mediator, individuals can interpret Scriptures for themselves, and anyone can preside at worship. But he too concludes that none of these functions are found in the

---

7. Hillyer, *1 and 2 Peter, Jude*, 71. Other OT references are also found in these verses. I have referred only to the ones directly related to our topic.

8. Elliott, "Elders as Leaders in 1 Peter and the Early Church," 551. Elliott goes further into the textual basis for this claim in *1 Peter*, 420.

9. Brown, *Priest and Bishop*, 14, 15.

text. Like Elliot and Brown, he asserts that the text refers to status, not function, although he does not explore the nature of this status.[10]

The other side of the debate argues that this passage does not (or at least, does not only) refer to status, but intends to communicate a functional dimension of this new priesthood. Eduard Schweizer argues that these verses do indeed include a functional dimension that goes beyond just a declaration of status, beyond a declaration that these people are elect. He argues that v. 9b sets forth the priestly function of proclamation. This function is given even more specificity: the proclamation is not intra-church, but is focused on the Gentiles. Schweizer does not see in these verses a reference to how the church should be structured,[11] but J. Ramsey Michaels does. Michaels argues that 1 Peter sets forth a mutuality (4:8–10) that should characterize the whole community. Michaels claims that 1 Pet 2:5, 9 should be understood in terms of this mutuality. He goes on to say that this mutuality excludes a hierarchy. All are called to the function of making spiritual sacrifices (2:5).[12] Michaels points to two specific functions of the priesthood: offering spiritual sacrifices (2:5) and proclaiming the mighty acts of God (2:9).[13] The latter is probably to be taken as the way in which the former is carried out. Similarly, G. W. Hansen connects 1 Pet 2:9 to the gifts talked about in 1 Pet 4:7–11. The function of the "royal priesthood" (2:9) is to use these gifts.[14]

After looking at this larger debate, we return now to the specific question regarding the activity of interpreting Scripture. If this priesthood has a functional dimension, does this function include the right of each individual to interpret Scripture for him/herself? I agree with Michaels, who, though he sees a functional dimension to this priesthood, says that this text simply does not indicate that the function of this priesthood has to do with the interpretation of Scripture.[15] This function might be established in other ways, but to do so on the basis of this passage is a shaky move.

---

10. Ferguson, *The Church of Christ*, 222.

11. Schweizer, "The Priesthood of All Believers," 292.

12. Michaels, *1 Peter*, 82–87. Although Michaels asserts that a hierarchy is ruled out, he does not take this to mean that differing roles in the congregation are ruled out.

13. Ibid., 13, 14.

14. Hansen, "Authority," 107.

15. Michaels, *1 Peter*, 13, 14.

The examination of 1 Peter 2:4–10 is important in discussing the priesthood of all believers for two reasons. First, this passage has played an important role in the theological discussion, especially since the Reformation. Second, the textual content is significant; the verses themselves are important to this discussion. The passage highlights a conception of priesthood that involves the whole people of God. Further details regarding the nature of this specific priesthood are difficult to ascertain from this passage, but Michaels is right in claiming that these verses should be understood in terms of the mutuality that Peter says should characterize the community. Though we need to draw on other texts as well to adequately ground a theology of the priesthood of all believers, this text provides a starting point for the discussion.

NT Patterns and Themes Related to the Priesthood of All Believers

Jewish Background

In the Jewish context, the central function of priests was to offer sacrifices on behalf of the people.[16] In the NT, the sacrificial role is not given to a priestly class but is handled in two ways. In Hebrews it is given exclusively to Christ (e.g., "Christ . . . offered for all time a single sacrifice for sins," [10:12]). Animal sacrifices are not carried forward into Christianity, but Christians are to offer spiritual sacrifices (Rom 12:1, 1 Pet 2:5).[17] The priestly activity of offering sacrifices, in the way that we see it carried into the early church, is an activity in which all believers are to engage, not just a priestly class.

The proclamation and interpretation of Torah was another priestly function in the Jewish context.[18] Like the function of sacrificing, this one is not reserved for a priestly class in the NT. Paul sees the functions of proclamation and interpretation as communal functions. He states that when the community gathers, *each one* has a lesson or an interpretation that should be offered for the building up of the community (1 Cor 14:26).

16. Basser, "Priests and Priesthood, Jewish," 73.

17. Romans 12:1 speaks of numerous "bodies," but these compose a singular sacrifice (not sacrifices)—the people as a whole make up the sacrifice. It is not a sacrifice that can be offered by each person in isolation from the community.

18. Gelpi notes, though, that by the first century, the function of interpreting the law had been largely taken over by the rabbis (*Committed Worship*, 73).

Some may be more gifted than others in these areas (1 Cor 12:28–30), but primary gifting is not equated with exclusive domain.

The Jewish priesthood was hereditary. Only those born into the lineage of Levi and Aaron could become priests. However, the book of Hebrews describes Jesus's priesthood as in the order of Melchizedek, not in the order of Levi. Jesus was a priest "through the power of an indestructible life" (Heb 7:13), not through a Levitical lineage. With Jesus, the hereditary nature of the priesthood comes to an end. While Christ's priesthood is unique, the priesthood to which Christians are called is also free from this hereditary dimension. Lineage is an unacceptable means of differentiation throughout the Christian community. Those who are born Gentiles are brought into the household of God; Jews and Gentiles are made into one group in Christ (Eph 2:11–22). Hereditary priestly roles are not found in the emerging church.

The NT shows that the early church drops the Jewish conception of priesthood. Sacrifice, proclamation, and interpretation were no longer reserved for a special class and hereditary duties from within Judaism were not carried forward into the church.

Specific Words

In the NT, the term *hiereus* (priest) is applied to Christ and to the whole people of God, but it is never used to designate an individual believer who has been set aside for ministry.[19] The book of Hebrews repeatedly refers to Jesus as the "high priest," and in Revelation the whole people of God are referred to as priests (Rev 1:6, 5:10, 20:6). But nowhere do we see an individual Christian or a subset of individuals designated as priests. Paul describes his work as "priestly service" (Rom 15:16) but this does not hint at the establishment of a priestly class within Christianity. In light of the fact that the term "priest" was commonly used in Judaism and so would have been well known to the NT writers, should we be surprised that this term is not taken up and applied to a narrowly defined Christian priest-

19. Many authors have made this observation. Alexandre Faivre provides a helpful discussion of the use of this term in *The Emergence of the Laity in the Early Church*, 7. For a supporting discussion of the same issue in a very different type of work, one which seeks to identify primary metaphors in the NT, see Bennett, *Metaphors of Ministry*, 103, 104. A work of a third type, one representing ecumenical dialogue, that sets forth this idea is "Ministry," in *Baptism, Eucharist, and Ministry*, 23 (hereafter referred to as BEM).

hood? Brown proposes that the early Christians saw the Jewish priests as their own, so there was no need to talk about a parallel Christian priesthood.[20] But this argument from silence does not overcome the other indicators that point to a rejection of the priestly system. The book of Hebrews shows that the early Christians believed that the priesthood system had come to an end in Christ; therefore they would consciously avoid the term. Also, as Donald Gelpi points out, the priestly caste was chiefly responsible for Jesus's death and so "it should, then, come as no surprise, that the first leaders of the Christian community felt loathe to take them as role models. We find, as a consequence, no indication within the New Testament of a priestly caste within the apostolic church similar to the Levitical priesthood."[21]

Isn't the idea of the laity found in the NT? And if so, doesn't this imply a contrasting priestly caste? Our English word "laity" is related to the Greek word *laos* but the meaning of the two words must not be equated. *Laos* means something significantly different from our word "laity." *Laos* is a common word in the NT and it has a range of meanings including "nation," "crowd," "population," and "people."[22] *Laos* never means a group of non-ordained people that is in contrast to a priestly group.[23] The NT usage of this word, unlike the English use of the word "laity," does not raise difficulties in regard to the doctrine of the priesthood of all believers. It does not create a sub-category of "non-ordained."

Another word related to this discussion is *kleros*, from which our word "clergy" is derived. The main meaning in the NT for *kleros* is the

20. Brown, *Priest and Bishop*, 17. For a full treatment of the types of leadership models in the first century upon which the early Christians could draw, see Clarke, *Serve the Community of the Church*.

21. Gelpi, *Committed Worship*, 77–78.

22. Strathmann, *TDNT* 4:50–57.

23. An example of how this point enters into the theological discussions can be seen in the Catholic theologians Lawler and Shanahan. In commenting on "*Lumen Gentium*," they agree with this understanding of *laos*. See Lawler and Shanahan, *Church: A Spirited Communion*, 5. Catholic theologian Giovanni Magnani provides an interesting discussion of the word *laos* and its adjectival derivative, *laikos*, which he translates "layperson." He argues, based on a 1958 article by I. de le Potterie, that in Greek usage, as far back as the third century BC, the adjective *laikos* refers to a crowd of people in contrast to their leaders. He goes on to argue that Congar and others were wrong in extending the meaning of *laos* to *laikos*. While the adjectival form may have this history, what I have said about the NT usage of the noun—and the significance of this for us—stands. See Magnani, "Does the So-Called Theology of the Laity Possess a Theological Status?" 570–72.

"portion allotted to someone."[24] A related word is used to describe someone who is chosen (Eph 1:11). Faivre observes that in the NT, *kleros* refers to all the people of God.[25] He notes that *kleros* never refers to a special priestly class.[26] The contemporary understanding of "clergy" differs greatly from its root word, *kleros*. This means, then, that *kleros* is used in a way similar to *laos*.

NT Congregations

Our hunt for patterns and themes must go beyond the examination of specific words. We must look also for congregational structures that might be evident in the clearly Pauline congregations, the congregations addressed by the Pastoral Epistles, and the congregations reflected in Acts.

What patterns do we see in the Pauline churches? Many hold that Paul argues for a charismatic rather than a hierarchical structure of the body.[27] As part of his argument, Paul claims that every member of the body is necessary and every member has a gift (Rom 12, 1 Cor 12).[28] C. K. Barrett asserts that it is clear from Rom 12 and 1 Cor 12 that Paul has no interest in office; Paul's interest is in function.[29]

Barrett goes on to make an insightful observation regarding Paul's admonitions to the Corinthian church in relation to the Lord's Supper (1 Cor 11). In addressing the abuses that were occurring, Paul does not call on any particular leader to enforce his dictums. His primary instruction is for the people in the congregation to wait for one another (1 Cor 11:33). Barrett suggests that no particular individual had the task of presiding at

24. Foerster, *TDNT* 3:763.

25. Faivre, *The Emergence of the Laity in the Early Church*, 7, 15.

26. Ibid.

27. For one of the pioneering presentations of this view, see Brunner, *The Misunderstanding of the Church*. In his important treatment of ecclesiastical authority, Hans von Campenhausen also sees the Holy Spirit as the organizing principle of the church for Paul. See Campenhausen, Ecclesiastical Authority, *Ecclesiastical Authority*, 58. The prominent NT scholar, James D. G. Dunn, asserts this position. See Dunn, *The Theology of Paul the Apostle*, 552. For an ecclesiology from a Catholic perspective that understands Paul in this way and promotes a pneumatological organization of the church, see Küng, *The Church*. The Reformed theologian Jürgen Moltmann also understands Paul this way. See Moltmann, *The Church in the Power of the Spirit*.

28. A full treatment of these charisms will be given in ch. 3.

29. Barrett, *Church, Ministry, and Sacraments in the New Testament*, 32.

the Lord's Supper, otherwise Paul would have told the people to simply wait until such a leader said to begin.[30] Paul did not call the people to come to order under the direction of an office holder because no such person existed in Corinth.

Paul refers to apostles, prophets, and teachers (1 Cor 12:28). How are these three identities to be understood? This has been the subject of great debate over the last century.[31] This debate is related to the fact that these identities are surprisingly marginal to Paul's concept of ministry.[32] One side of the debate holds that these are three *functions* and that the Pauline churches operated democratically.[33] The other side of the debate argues that these identities amount to administrative offices at the local level, which functioned simultaneously with a charismatic organization at the level of the whole church.[34] Dunn holds that we should take Paul's vision of the charismatic nature of the church as fundamental to his ecclesiology.[35] Dunn's view rejects the idea that Paul sought to institute a set pattern of church authority and structure.

The Pastoral Epistles have played an important role in the discussion of office and thus in the discussion of the priesthood of all believers. What patterns or themes emerge in these letters? Here elders are appointed (Titus 1:5), this appointment is to a group composed of a number of other elders (1 Tim 4:14), and the qualifications of bishops and deacons are set forth (1 Tim 3). Do these letters set a normative structure for the church? If so, some understandings of the priesthood of all believers would be ruled out.

G. W. Hansen claims that the Pastoral Epistles represent the most developed form of church structure in the NT.[36] He states that in 1 and 2 Timothy we see not the universal distribution of charisms typical of Paul, but the bestowal of the charism of office through ordination. According to Hansen, some claim that the presence of this structure fortifies the argument that these letters were not written by Paul, while others do not

---

30. Ibid., 33.

31. See Dunn, *The Theology of Paul the Apostle*, 566–71.

32. Ibid., 566.

33. Ibid.

34. Ibid., 567.

35. Ibid., 598.

36. Hansen, "Authority," 105.

attribute the different tone to a difference in authorship but to a difference in the historical context being addressed—apparently the church was in crisis and this required a more defined structure.[37] Von Campenhausen is one who has argued for the latter position. He claims that in the face of Gnostic challenges, clear, authoritative leadership was needed.[38] A third explanation for the more structured picture of the church that appears in the letters to Timothy is that these letters represent a later stage of development in the life of the church.[39] According to this view, when the expectation for the immanent return of Christ began to fade, the churches began to shift from a charismatic organization to a more hierarchical organization to ensure their long-term viability. Those who argue today for a more structured ecclesiology tend to view the Pastorals in this developmental way and take these later developments as normative.[40] Von Campenhausen rejects this developmental view and argues that the variations in structure should be primarily attributed to geographical location.[41] Hansen also rejects this developmental view. He points out that in the writings from the late first and early second centuries a range of approaches existed. Some congregations were indeed becoming more hierarchical but others persistently resisted this institutional thrust.[42] It has been proposed that the more structured tenor of the Pastorals is due to these particular congregations importing Jewish authority structures, whereas other NT congregations had not.[43] On the whole, von Campenhausen and Hansen seem to be right in their assessments: from what we can ascertain regarding the early church, we cannot say one uniform, normative pattern of development existed.

We turn now to the church in Acts. Dunn states that there are two main views of how the church in Acts was organized. One view is that here we have a definite organizational structure.[44] The twelve apostles were the primary leaders in the Jerusalem community (e.g., Acts 1:15–26; 2:42; 4:32–37). A second office was created to assist the apostles with

---

37. Ibid., 105, 106.

38. Campenhausen, *Ecclesiastical Authority*, 117.

39. Faivre, *The Emergence of the Laity in the Early Church*, 10, 11.

40. Ferguson, *The Church of Christ*, 309.

41. Campenhausen, *Ecclesiastical Authority*, 120.

42. Hansen, "Authority," 105.

43. Campenhausen, *Ecclesiastical Authority*, 116.

44. James D. G. Dunn, *Unity and Diversity in the New Testament*, 106–7.

administrative chores (Acts 6:1–6). Elders are said to constitute a third office, one that shares authority with the apostles (e.g., Acts 15:2, 4, 6, 22–35). Some have correlated the apostles with bishops, the elders with priests, and the administrative assistants with deacons.[45] According to this reading, in Acts we have an early form of Catholicism.[46] But Dunn suggests this view has a number of problems. First, the apostles are constituted by more than just the twelve, and their mission was not to stay in Jerusalem as leaders, but to go out as missionaries.[47] Second, the selection of the seven to assist the disciples was more a recognition of authority they already had rather than an installation to office.[48] Third, while elders play an important part in the Jerusalem church, they are not mentioned as part of the Pauline churches until the Pastoral Epistles, which reflect a time later in the church's development. So if we read the Pauline material along with Acts we get the sense that Luke was likely seeking to portray the role of elders as more solidified in the broader church than the role actually was when he wrote.[49]

A second main view, the one Dunn himself holds, is that leadership and authority in the early church as seen in Acts was spontaneous and diverse.[50] Often ministry was undertaken without the authorization of other leaders. Rather, in case after case, it was carried out under the guidance and authority of the Holy Spirit (e.g., Paul and Barnabas in Acts 13:2; Stephen in Acts 6:8,10; the Jerusalem council in Acts 15:28). Rather than pointing to a developing ecclesial structure, this view sees Acts as pointing to a leadership that was spontaneous and charismatic.

This NT overview shows the ecclesiological significance of the royal priesthood. To summarize, a hierarchy is nowhere mandated or made normative. At no point in the NT are the responsibilities of the universal priesthood caste in individualistic terms. We are given *no* indication that each person is his or her *own* priest, the significance of which will be highlighted in the theological discussion below. Nowhere in the NT is a cultic priesthood seen to be part of the early church and nowhere

---

45. Ibid., 107.

46. Hansen, "Authority," 106.

47. Dunn, *Unity and Diversity in the New Testament*, 107.

48. Ibid.

49. Ibid., 108.

50. Ibid.

in the NT is the word "priest" applied to any individual in any church. And in contrast with some claims, even as the church developed, a variety of leadership patterns existed. No normative pattern can be construed even from the later NT writings. What this all means is that a hierarchical ecclesiology is not mandated, and in fact, seems to stand against the participatory and pneumatological patterns seen in many of these texts. The functions of sacrifice, proclamation, and interpretation that were associated with the Levitical priesthood are now given to the universal priesthood of believers. We do not have in the NT the establishment of a separated ministerial priesthood; rather, we have a single priesthood composed of *all* Christians. But we cannot stop here. Do *theological* reasons exist that validate the establishment of a second priesthood? I take up this question in chapter three, but first, in the next section I show the contours of the current theological discussion.

THEOLOGICAL DISCUSSIONS REGARDING THE PRIESTHOOD OF ALL BELIEVERS

In this section, I will highlight key historical turning points in the discussion of the priesthood of all believers. Then I will look more closely at the conversations that have taken place from the 1960s to the present. In my treatment of these more recent conversations, I will include Catholic, ecumenical, and Free Church approaches to the issue. After highlighting selected Free Church voices, I will look in more depth at the ideas of Free Church theologians John Howard Yoder and Miroslav Volf.

Historical Turning Points

Though the NT churches did not have a concept of "laity" as a group distinct from ministers, this understanding gradually took root and became widely held in the church. Clement of Rome, writing at the end of the first century, appears to be the first Christian writer to make a distinction between laity and clergy, but the term "laity" continued to be uncommon well into the second century.[51] Rather quickly after this, though, clergy became identified as the ones who did the ministry in the church, an identification that became entrenched in the following centuries.

51. Faivre, Faivre, *The Emergence of the Laity in the Early Church*, 15, 25.

The most important turning point in the history of this doctrine came with the Reformation. In Timothy George's view, Luther's greatest contribution to Protestant ecclesiology was the doctrine of the priesthood of all believers.[52] While I must assert again that the idea certainly precedes Luther (see NT discussion above), Luther did indeed make a significant ecclesiological contribution by lifting up the royal priesthood anew.

Luther believed that every Christian is part of the priesthood. He wanted all Christians to know that "all of us alike are priests, and that we all have the same authority in regard to the Word and the Sacraments, although no one has the right to administer them without the consent of the members of his Church, and the call of the majority."[53] According to Paul Althaus, Luther ascribed two main functions to this priesthood. One function is to proclaim the word of God.[54] George asserts that while Luther saw proclamation as the highest office in the church, Luther did not see it as an office reserved for a few; rather, he saw it as an office in which all Christians participate.[55] Luther stated, "a Christian not only has the right but the duty to teach the word of God; and he fails to do so at the risk of his own salvation."[56] The other function of all Christians as priests is to hear confessions and to offer forgiveness.[57] Every Christian has the authority to do this.

Luther's view was that Christians are priests for each other: they proclaim the word to each other, intercede with God on behalf of each other, and offer sacrifices on behalf of each other.[58] This is an important point, because it is distinct from the view that has arisen in some circles which claims that because each Christian is a priest, therefore each Christian can carry out the priestly functions for him/herself. Greg Ogden, among others, takes Luther to say that we are our *own* priests in addition to be-

---

52. George, *Theology of the Reformers*, 95.

53. Quoted in Eastwood, *The Priesthood of All Believers*, 6.

54. Althaus, *The Theology of Martin Luther*, 315.

55. George, *Theology of the Reformers*, 97.

56. Quoted in Althaus, *The Theology of Martin Luther*, 315. At the same time, Luther did reserve the public proclamation of the word for those who have been appointed to do so by the community, but Luther did not see this difference in expression as creating a separate priesthood. See Althaus, *The Theology of Martin Luther*, 315, 325.

57. Althaus, *The Theology of Martin Luther*, 316–17.

58. Ibid., 314.

ing priests to each other.[59] One must question whether this is an accurate reading of Luther, however. While Luther does assert that we are all priests, and he is clear that we are priests for each other, he does *not* say that we are our *own* priests. Luther does not suggest that I as a Christian should proclaim the word to myself, or that I should hear my own confessions. The view that we are our own priests normally is put forth to assert that we are all competent to come before God without mediators. This is a valid and important assertion, yet it does not say enough. Others *do* in fact mediate on a regular basis between God and a given Christian. Christians come to God on behalf of a brother or sister and speak to the brother or sister on behalf of God. The priestly role has an individual dimension, but it cannot be properly conceived of in purely individual terms. To read such an individualistic and isolationist view into Luther is anachronistic. Luther had no intention of framing the doctrine in such terms.

Luther's view of the priesthood of all believers did not rule out church office. In fact, Luther saw the ministerial office as essential; office is one of the signs of the church's presence.[60] Yet the ministerial office is not completely distinct from the priesthood of all believers. It actually does not differ in content and authority from the priesthood of all believers.[61] What *is* different is the public character of the ministerial office. While all Christians are to proclaim the word and to offer forgiveness, Luther held that those in ministerial office do this on behalf of the entire community.[62]

Calvin did not emphasize this doctrine to the extent Luther did, but neither did he ignore it. He stressed that Christ is the only high priest and he held that through Christ's substitutionary priesthood the people of God are formed into a priesthood.[63] Calvin's view of the priesthood of all believers was also tied to his understanding of calling. Each person has a divine calling, and as people follow their calling, they are priests in their daily vocations.[64] Like Luther, Calvin saw an important role for the ministerial priesthood. In contrast with the Catholic Church from which

---

59. Ogden, *Unfinished Business*, 17.

60. Althaus, *The Theology of Martin Luther*, 323.

61. Ibid., 326.

62. Ibid., 327.

63. Eastwood, *The Priesthood of All Believers*, 68.

64. Ibid., 73.

he was departing, Calvin saw these ministers as within rather than above the universal priesthood.[65]

The Anabaptists did not give sustained doctrinal attention to the priesthood of all believers as did Luther, and yet their lived theology took the priesthood of all believers further than Luther and the Magisterial Reformers. At his interrogation in 1527, the Anabaptist, Ambrosius Spitelmaier, when asked what the Anabaptists did when they came together, responded in part by saying, "When they have come together they teach one another the divine Word and one asks the other: how do you understand this saying?"[66] This mutuality in the teaching of Scripture was not the norm in the Reformers' churches or in the Catholic Church. Another example of an Anabaptist view comes from an early Anabaptist tract that includes these words: "When some one comes to church and constantly hears only one person speaking, and all the listeners are silent, neither speaking nor prophesying, who can or will regard or confess the same to be a spiritual congregation, or confess according to 1 Cor 14 that God is indwelling and operating in them through his Holy Spirit with his gifts, impelling them one after the other in the above mentioned order of speaking and prophesying?"[67] The assumption was that the congregation as a whole should be involved in proclaiming the word when the community gathered. The voices of the early Anabaptists were not in complete unity on this issue, yet the overall thrust was for an ecclesiology that actively involved all the people and had little regard for clerical office. The Anabaptist perspective was of minimal influence at the time, but I include it here because it is an important seedbed of the Free Church tradition, which is widespread today.

Each century since the Reformation has seen the doctrine of the universal priesthood taken up in different ways, primarily by renewal movements. The Puritan tradition, which emerged in the second half of the sixteenth century, gave birth in the seventeenth century to the Baptists and the Quakers, both of which have held a form of the doctrine of the priesthood of all believers in high regard.[68] The eighteenth century saw the rise of Methodism. Its founder, John Wesley, held a theology of the

65. Ibid., 90.

66. Quoted in Klaassen, *Anabaptism in Outline*, 124.

67. Ibid., 127.

68. Eastwood, *The Priesthood of All Believers*, 130, 131.

priesthood of all believers that was similar to Luther's.[69] Wesley can be distinguished from Luther, however, in the area of application. Wesley went far beyond Luther in implementing the priesthood of all believers. Cyril Eastwood, in his two-part work on the history of the priesthood of all believers, states in rather dramatic terms, "the most thoroughgoing application of these basic principles that has ever been attempted in the history of Christendom was undertaken by John Wesley."[70] Wesley's emphasis on lay involvement in ministry influenced the parachurch movements that began to emerge in the second half of the nineteenth century (e.g., The YMCA and the Student Volunteer Movement).[71]

As the twentieth century unfolded this theme of lay involvement continued to develop as evidenced in the work of John Mott, a key leader of the student movement and the ecumenical movement.[72] His book *Liberating the Lay Forces of Christianity* was a groundbreaking work when it came out in 1932 because so little had been written on the topic prior to this time and because his voice had credibility in a range of traditions as a result of his pioneering work on inter-church dialogue.[73] The voice of the French Catholic ecclesiologist and ecumenist, Yves Congar, came to the fore in Catholic discussions of the laity. His book *Lay People in the Church*, first published in 1953,[74] was significant within Catholic circles (and beyond) because he was arguably the first prominent theologian within the tradition to give a sustained treatment to the importance of the laity.[75] Congar's participation in the preparatory theological commission for Vatican II is reflected in the shape of the final documents to emerge from that council.[76] The Dutch Reformed theologian and missiologist Hendrik Kraemer, through his 1958 book *A Theology of the Laity*,[77] made a significant contribution to the ecumenical discussion of the laity by providing a

---

69. Ibid., 193.

70. Ibid., 203.

71. Ahlstrom, *A Religious History of the American People*, 742, 865.

72. Tomkins, "Mott, John R.," 704.

73. Mott, *Liberating the Lay Forces of Christianity*.

74. The English translation was first published in 1957. See Congar, *Lay People in the Church*.

75. For a helpful treatment of the development of Congar's theology of the laity, see Pellitero, "Congar's Developing Understanding of the Laity and Their Mission."

76. Stransky, "Congar, Yves," 217.

77. Kraemer, *A Theology of the Laity*.

solid theological foundation for the growing number of people who were encouraging lay involvement in the church.[78] Writing from within the Quaker tradition, Elton Trueblood was one of the most significant and prolific writers on the American scene to champion the laity during the middle decades of the twentieth century. In one of his early works, *Your Other Vocation*, he pushed for work and family life to be understood as ministry contexts, thus broadening the category of "minister" to include all Christians.[79] Throughout his works he emphasized that the modern distinction between clergy and laity was disjunctive with the NT witness and he argued that the church should be viewed as a company of the committed[80] or a society of ministers,[81] an ecclesiology that pointed up the relational and participatory nature of the church.

The 1960s and 1970s proved to be a fertile time for considering the role of the laity in the church. In Protestant circles, some of the key figures who were bringing about a renewal of the priesthood of all believers include Gordon Cosby, Richard Mouw, William Diehl, Robert Coleman, Ray Stedman, and Howard Snyder.[82] In Catholicism, the key event in relation to this discussion was the convening of Vatican II, an event that had ramifications far beyond the Catholic tradition. It is to Vatican II and Catholic theology that we now turn.

Vatican II and the Ministry of the Whole People of God

The Second Vatican Council, which met from 1962–1965, marks a major milestone in Catholic theology. Prior to Vatican II, Catholic ecclesiology focused much more on the role of priests than on the role of the laity, and the role of priests was defined primarily in relation to the Eucharist.[83] A growing emphasis in Catholic theology on the pneumatological nature of the church led to an appreciation of the gifts of the Spirit that are distrib-

---

78. He appreciated the important work of Congar, but Kraemer felt the need to add to the emerging discussion on behalf of non-Catholic Christians. Cf. Ibid., 11.

79. Trueblood, *Your Other Vocation*.

80. Trueblood, *The Company of the Committed*.

81. Trueblood, *The Incendiary Fellowship*, 39.

82. Cf. Dever, "The Priesthood of All Believers: Reconsidering Every-Member Ministry," for a perspective on the key figures in this time period.

83. McGreal, "Developments since Vatican II: A Roman Catholic Perspective," 113.

uted to all believers, an emphasis which allowed for a significantly different view of the role that the laity plays in the mission of the church.[84]

The most important Vatican II document for this discussion, and arguably the most important one to come out of Vatican II, is *Lumen Gentium* (The Dogmatic Constitution of the Church). The focus of *Lumen Gentium* is on how God's people are related within the church.

An understanding of the terminology used in *Lumen Gentium* will nuance our conception of the way Vatican II viewed the priesthood of all believers. Miguel Garijo-Guembe points out that *Lumen Gentium* does not use the phrase "priesthood of all believers," a phrase that he says was avoided because of its association with the anti-hierarchy sentiments of the Reformation.[85] The term "universal priesthood" is not used either, Peter Drilling notes.[86] This was because some council members argued that only Christ's priesthood could be described as universal. While in general Catholic theologians are not averse to using this last phrase, Drilling observes that Vatican II settled on the phrase "common priesthood" as a way of referring to the priesthood that is shared by all baptized (Roman?) Christians.[87]

We gain further theological insight by looking at the drafting process of *Lumen Gentium*. As noted earlier, the council wanted to encourage the laity to take a more active role in the church. One way the council fathers sought to do this was by setting forth the priestly dignity of all baptized people.[88] Another way this was done was through the ordering of the chapters. An early draft of this document had its second chapter as "On the Hierarchy" and its third chapter as "On the People of God and especially the Laity."[89] But the council made major revisions to better em-

---

84. Kärkkäinen, "The Calling of the Whole People of God into Ministry," 147. The mission of the laity is the focus of *Apostolicam Actuositatem*. I will focus primarily on *Lumen Gentium* because of its importance in setting forth the relationship of the common and ministerial priesthoods, and thus its importance for a theology of the priesthood of all believers. In 1989 another document on the laity, *Christifideles Laici* was issued. It builds on the teachings of Vatican II. See John Paul II, *Post-Synodal Apostolic Exhortation*.

85. Garijo-Guembe, *Communion of the Saints*, 134.

86. Drilling, "Common and Ministerial Priesthood," 85.

87. Ibid.

88. Ibid., 83. Whether this includes only Catholics or includes also those baptized in other traditions is an important question, but it is beyond the scope of this discussion.

89. Ibid. 84.

phasize the commonality of all the faithful. In the final version, the section on the whole people of God is treated separately from the laity, and it is placed in front of the treatment of the hierarchy. This order—the whole people of God first, followed by the hierarchy and the laity—emphasizes the unity of the people of God before going on to address differences.

Lumen Gentium picks up on a number of biblical images to show the importance of the whole people of God. This people is described as the body of Christ, with Christ as the head; the new Israel; a holy priesthood; and a kingdom of priests.[90] The importance of the whole people of God is emphasized also by the assertion that all believers share in the prophetic office of Christ.[91] They carry out the duties of this office by bearing witness to God through the use of the charisms granted by the Holy Spirit.[92] In the section on the laity, *Lumen Gentium* states that it is not only the prophetic office of Christ that is common to all, but the priestly and kingly offices as well.[93]

In what may be taken as a summary statement, *Lumen Gentium* posits that "everything that has been said of the People of God is addressed equally to laity, religious, and clergy."[94] However, Vatican II in no way sets forth an egalitarian view of the church. While many commonalities exist among all the faithful, definite differences exist also. A closer look at Vatican II's idea of charisms is helpful here.

Miguel María Garijo-Guembe suggests that underlying the council's statements on charisms[95] is the understanding that the charisms are of two types, a view not uncommon among Catholic theologians. One type is composed of those charisms that the Holy Spirit freely grants to individuals as the Spirit wills. A second type is made up of the charisms of office that individuals receive through ordination.[96] That all the faithful are part of the universal priesthood does not exclude a second type of priesthood, the ministerial priesthood. This differentiation of charisms

---

90. "*Lumen Gentium*," §9, §10.

91. Ibid., §12.

92. Ibid.

93. Ibid.

94. Ibid., §30. "*Presbyterorum Ordinis*" likewise emphasizes the commonality of all the faithful by saying "there is no such thing as a member that has not a share in the mission of the whole Body." See "*Presbyterorum Ordinis*," §2.

95. For example, "*Apostolicam Actuositatem*," §3. Also, "*Lumen Gentium*," §12.

96. Garijo-Guembe, *Communion of the Saints*, 137.

can be seen readily in the eucharist where only those with the charism of office—bishops (or priests as their representatives)—can preside.[97]

Lumen Gentium contains two texts that are particularly crucial to this discussion. The first comes from the section on the whole people of God and serves as a not-so-subtle reminder that this section is not to be misconstrued as undercutting the hierarchy. This text says that all the baptized are part of a holy priesthood and then goes on to say:

> Though they differ essentially and not only in degree, the common priesthood of the faithful and the ministerial or hierarchical priesthood are none the less ordered one to another; each in its own proper way shares in the one priesthood of Christ.[98]

Much discussion has centered on the use here of the word "essentially" and what this means for the relationship between the common and ministerial priesthoods. Vatican II used the word here and in other documents, but nowhere did the council define the word.[99] A number of Catholic theologians since then have taken up this task.[100] We will not enter into the technical aspects of this discussion, but suffice it to say that the wording at a minimum affirms certain functions and roles for the clergy that are not shared by the laity. The text moves toward differentiation.

A second key text moves in the other way: toward commonality. Although it receives much less attention, Miguel Garijo-Guembe observes that this text was the subject of one of the most important discussions of Vatican II.[101] It states that because the whole people of God participates in Christ's prophetic office,

97. "*Lumen Gentium,*" §26, §28. For an in-depth look at the justification for the way Vatican II relates the common and ordained priesthoods, see Coffey, "The Common and the Ordained Priesthood." For a different perspective on Vatican II's theological justification for the ministerial priesthood, which comes by way of a critique of Coffey, see Welch, "For the Church and within the Church."

98. "*Lumen Gentium,*" §10.

99. Kenan B. Osborne, *Priesthood : A History of Ordained Ministry in the Roman Catholic Church* (New York: Paulist Press, 1989), 341. This book is particularly helpful in further unpacking Vatican II's view of the relationship between the priesthood and the laity.

100. For a thorough treatment of the background and meaning of this sentence and specifically of the way "essentially" is used here, see Drilling, "Common and Ministerial Priesthood." For another helpful treatment of this text which moves in the direction of more constructive theology, see Coffey.

101. Garijo-Guembe, *Communion of the Saints,* 136.

> The whole body of the faithful who have an anointing that comes from the holy one (cf. 1 Jn. 2:20 and 27) cannot err in matters of belief. This characteristic is shown in the supernatural appreciation of the faith (*sensus fidei*) of the whole people, when, "from the bishops to the last of the faithful" [Augustine] they manifest a universal consent in matters of faith and morals. By this appreciation of the faith, aroused and sustained by the Spirit of truth, the People of God, guided by the sacred teaching authority (*magisterium*), and obeying it, receives not the mere word of men, but truly the word of God (cf. 1 Th. 2:13), the faith once for all delivered to the saints (cf. Jude 3).[102]

This text makes a powerful statement about the whole people of God: the faith of the body as a whole is infallible. To the chagrin of the conservative council fathers, this statement reversed the order which had been the norm since Vatican I. The general approach of Vatican I was to put first the infallibility of the teaching office and then to speak of the faith of the people as something that the people received passively from this office. But Vatican II set forth first the infallible nature of the faith of the whole people of God. This faith remains under the guidance of the teaching office, but it is not simply deduced from it.[103] This statement gives great value to the whole people of God, the priesthood of all believers, and is oriented towards commonality, although differentiation is not eliminated.

Today, some forty years after Vatican II, these documents retain a surprising freshness. They continue to be foundational for an ongoing discussion within the Catholic communion regarding the nature of the common and the ministerial priesthoods.

This ongoing discussion has two main parts: 1) a consideration of the ontological nature of each of these priesthoods, which leads to 2) a consideration of the relationship between these two priesthoods. The main approach taken by Catholic theologians has been to ground both priesthoods Christologically in the headship and priesthood of Christ.[104] Peter Drilling assumes this Christological approach and goes on to argue that the relationship between the two priesthoods should be understood

---

102. "*Lumen Gentium*," §12.

103. This discussion is based on the observations of Garijo-Guembe, *Communion of the Saints*, 136, 137.

104. Coffey, "The Common and the Ordained Priesthood," 210.

analogically, that is, the common priesthood is related analogically to the ministerial priesthood.[105]

In contrast to Drilling, David Coffey argues that this Christological grounding does not adequately reflect Vatican II. Coffey points out that while these priesthoods are grounded in the priesthood of Christ, Christ's priesthood is expressed by the Holy Spirit through the church. Therefore Christ's priesthood is more properly referenced pneumatologically and expressed ecclesiologically, with Christological connections being secondary.[106] Vatican II grounds the ordained priesthood Christologically, and thus, argues Coffey, this priesthood continues to be lifted out of the church, leaving only the common priesthood to be understood ecclesiologically (and not Christologically).[107] Coffey argues that statements within the Vatican II documents provide for another way of grounding the ordained priesthood. Coffey points to statements that highlight the pneumatological ground of both the ordained and the common priesthood.[108] He contends that grounding both of these priesthoods pneumatologically and ecclesiologically shows how these two priesthoods are related.[109] Their essential difference, according to Coffey, lies in the fact that the common priesthood derives from the sacrament of baptism and is a "dynamism of faith"[110] while the ministerial priesthood derives from the charism of office given sacramentally through ordination.[111]

While Coffey's article has been widely affirmed in recent discussions of priestly representation,[112] Lawrence Welch argues that Coffey's central claims are not solid. Welch's primary point of attack is Coffey's assertion that Vatican II did not ground the common priesthood Christologically. In taking on Coffey, Welsh asserts that "a careful reading of *Lumen Gentium* cannot sustain the interpretation that Vatican II presented the common priesthood as directly ecclesiological and only indirectly Christological."[113] This leads to Welsh's challenge of a second of Coffey's claims: that refer-

---

105. Drilling, "Common and Ministerial Priesthood," 89–90.

106. Coffey, "The Common and the Ordained Priesthood," 210–25 passim.

107. Ibid., 224–25.

108. Ibid., 211–34 passim.

109. Ibid., 235.

110. Ibid., 228.

111. Ibid., 210, 227, 228.

112. Welch, "For the Church and within the Church," 613 n. 1.

113. Ibid., 622.

encing the ministerial priesthood Christologically elevates it above the church. Welsh argues that ordained priests should not only be seen in direct relationship to the headship of Christ (contra Coffey), but he argues that they should at once be seen ecclesiologically as well. Their connection with the headship of Christ does not remove them from the church because such headship has no meaning outside the church; the headship of Christ can be expressed only through the church.[114]

Vatican II did much to promote the whole people of God, but at the same time Vatican II set forth clear demarcations between the common and ordained priesthoods. The way in which it framed the nature of and the relationship between the ministerial and common priesthoods continues to be the subject of ongoing discussions within the Catholic communion. I have a great appreciation for the documents of Vatican II and for the tradition, and yet on this issue I chart a different course. I welcome Vatican II's emphasis on the charismatic nature of the church; this charismatic nature is the basis of my view of the priesthood of all believers. However, as I will show in the next chapter, my understanding of this charismatic nature leads me to different conclusions.

Ecumenical Discussions

In relation to the priesthood of all believers, the most important document in the current phase of the ecumenical discussion is *Baptism, Eucharist and Ministry* (BEM), put out in 1982 by the Faith and Order Commission of the World Council of Churches. This document has proved to be of enormous value for two reasons. First, it represents a significant ecumenical effort, and second, it serves as a fixed point for dialogue for a whole range of churches, akin to the role of Vatican II documents for Catholics.

The section of particular relevance for our discussion is the third chapter, "Ministry." Like *Lumen Gentium*, this chapter begins by speaking of the whole people of God.[115] The Holy Spirit brings the community of all believers into existence. The Spirit distributes diverse and complementary gifts to those in the body. The Holy Spirit gives every believer a charism and all are involved in the ministry of God.[116] BEM looks at the whole

114. Ibid., 631.

115. BEM §I.

116. Ibid., §II.7. These emphases on the whole people of God, the pneumatological nature of the church, and the gifts of the Spirit are also found in the more recent Faith

people of God before turning to ordination because it is out of the whole people of God that ordination arises.

From within the whole people of God, certain people are called to a more specific form of ministry. These ministers or priests are appointed by ordination.[117] Ordained ministers are needed in order for the church to fulfill its mission.[118] The document then goes on to give a justification for the existence of office.[119] BEM acknowledges that the words "priest" and "priesthood" are never used in the NT to designate ordained ministry,[120] but claims that "since very early times" the church has ordained people,[121] or at least "the basic reality of ordained ministry was present from the beginning."[122] The church as a whole derives its priestly character from the priesthood of Christ.[123] Like the whole people of God, ordained ministers are related to the priesthood of Christ and the priesthood of the church, but the ordained differ from the laity because they perform priestly activities.[124]

While BEM does affirm the priesthood of all believers, some churches have claimed that this section on ministry focuses almost entirely on the ordained priesthood and neglects the ministry of the laity.[125] This perhaps reveals the underlying theological positions of those who had primary responsibility for drafting the document, though in fairness I must note that the purpose of the document was to outline points of commonality, and so the exact nature of the ministry of the non-ordained was not central.

Additionally, some have claimed that BEM sets forth a view of ministry that assumes a certain sacramental theology which hints at the idea that ordination imparts an "indelible character." This would point in the direction of an ontological difference between the ordained and non-

---

and Order document, *The Nature and Purpose of the Church.*

117. BEM §II.8.

118. Ibid.

119. Ibid., §II.9–§II.14.

120. Ibid., §II. Commentary (§17).

121. Ibid., §II.8.

122. Ibid., §II. Commentary (§11).

123. Ibid., §II.17.

124. Ibid.

125. For example, see the Church of the Brethren response in Thurian, ed., *Churches Respond to BEM*, vol. VI, 110.

ordained. The United Methodists, for one, have expressed ambivalence regarding this issue in *BEM*.[126]

These critiques may be valid, and yet the positive value of *BEM* must not be swept aside. *BEM* is the first major ecumenical document to give the laity a prominent place in the discussion of the church. *BEM* undertook the dubious task of steering a middle course between Catholic and Protestant views, and must be judged a success in spite of the inevitable shortcomings of such an attempt. One great value of *BEM* is that it provides a whole range of churches with a fixed, common starting point for critical dialogue. This dialogue has pointed up that the ecumenical discussion needs to be developed further in relation to the priesthood of all believers.

A Selection of Free Church Voices

The Baptist theologian Carlyle Marney stands in the line of those who seek renewal in the church. He argues, in a way similar to Vatican II, that the whole people of God is needed to carry out God's redemptive mission.[127] He emphasizes that this redemption is a redemption of the world, not of the church. Its broadness requires a new priesthood and he sees a new Reformation at hand that is bringing about this priesthood. Like Luther, Marney's emphasis is on the idea that we are priests to each other.[128] He does not take this doctrine in an individualistic direction.

Herschel Hobbs, another Baptist, explicitly rejects the idea that we are priests to each other.[129] He rejects this based on a theology of the competency of the soul, a theology that he identifies as a key Baptist contribution to the church.[130] Hobbs emphasizes that each person is competent to stand before God without a mediator. Each person has the ability to choose for or against God. According to Hobbs, the idea that we are priests to each other undercuts this doctrine of direct, personal responsibility and access. In his view, the claim that we are priests to each other cannot be reconciled with the belief that each person has soul competency. Hobbs is

126. Thurian, ed., *Churches Respond to BEM*, vol. II, 196.

127. Marney, *Priests to Each Other*, 3.

128. Ibid., 5–7.

129. Hobbs, *You Are Chosen*, 14.

130. Ibid., 1–4, 14.

representative of an individualistic interpretation of the priesthood of all believers. In fact, he and others alter the phrase by making it singular. He refers to "the priesthood of the believer."

Like Hobbs, Timothy George relates the doctrine of soul competency to the priesthood of all believers. But unlike Hobbs, George argues that we are *not* our own priests, but rather, with Luther, he argues that we are priests *to* each other.[131] He states that soul competency has to do with individual responsibility. Like Hobbs, George understands soul competency as meaning that every person, whether Christian or not, is responsible for his or her response to God. But George argues that this has more to do with a person's status, while the doctrine of the priesthood of all believers has to do with a person's service.[132] I agree with George that our being priests to each other does not undercut our responsibility before God for our own actions.

In 1988 the Southern Baptist Convention passed the *Resolution on the Priesthood of the Believer*, a resolution whose title shows the shift to the singular seen above in Hobbs. This is an astounding resolution because it dramatically departs from Baptist tradition by shifting the ecclesial distribution of responsibility from the whole people toward the elders or pastors. It emphasizes the authority of leaders and cautions that "the doctrine of the priesthood of the believer can be used to justify the undermining of pastoral authority in the local church."[133] In contrast with the traditional Baptist emphasis, the resolution seeks to centralize power. It affirms a belief in what it calls "the biblical doctrine of the priesthood of the believer," but whatever this might mean, it "in no way contradicts the biblical understanding of the role, responsibility, and authority of the pastor which is seen in the command to the local church in Hebrews 13:17, 'Obey your leaders, and submit to them; for they keep watch over your souls, as those who will give an account.'"[134] In one fell swoop, this resolution cuts the legs out from under the traditional Baptist emphasis on, and understanding of, the priesthood of all believers.

---

131. George, *Theology of the Reformers*, 96. See also George, "The Priesthood of All Believers," 92.

132. George, "The Priesthood of All Believers," 92.

133. *Resolution on the Priesthood of the Believer*. I find it rather astonishing that such a resolution was passed.

134. Ibid.

This resolution by no means speaks for all Southern Baptists. Walter Shurden in *Proclaiming the Baptist Vision: The Priesthood of All Believers* has put together a collection of responses to the resolution; Shurden himself argues that this resolution distorts Baptist history. While the resolution argues otherwise, Shurden asserts that the high profile of the doctrine of the priesthood of all believers *has* been important in Baptist history and is *not* a recent development.[135] Shurden also argues that, contrary to what the resolution claims, the major Baptist theologians referred to in the resolution *did indeed* give significant attention to this doctrine.[136] Shurden reasserts positively several dimensions of the doctrine of the priesthood of all believers. He lists five: all have access to God, this access is personal and un-coerced, all share this privilege equally, responsibility for ministry is shared by all, it includes a universal dimension because all believers are given gifts for ministry, and it calls for religious liberty, that is, the ability to choose one's own religion without interference by the state.[137] This list faithfully reflects the main content that has traditionally been given to the doctrine of the priesthood of all believers.

In this same collection, Nancy Ammerman argues that the doctrine set forth by Luther and the other Reformers had a corporate tone that is in stark contrast to the individualistic tone of the resolution. She states that the Reformers "never envisioned solo believers standing figuratively alone before God in prayer and Bible reading. They talked about the priesthood of *all* believers, emphasizing the equality, not the aloneness."[138]

While the last several decades have seen much positive attention given to the priesthood of all believers, this resolution by the Southern Baptists shows that the way forward has not been without significant obstacles.

---

135. Shurden, "The Priesthood of All Believers and Pastoral Authority," 149–151.

136. Ibid.

137. Shurden, "Introduction," 3. Interestingly, the Catholic theologian, Hans Küng, has set forth a similar list. He states that the concrete content of the priesthood of all believers includes, 1) direct access to God, 2) making spiritual sacrifices, 3) preaching the word, 4) administering baptism, the Lord's supper, and the forgiveness of sins, and 5) mediating functions (because the first four are all done in service of others, not on one's own behalf). See Küng, *The Church*, 327–81.

138. Ammerman, "Priests and Prophets," 56.

The United Methodist, Gayle Carlton Felton, argues that the priesthood of all believers needs to be understood broadly.[139] She holds that this priesthood does indeed include the idea that each person can access God directly without a mediator. But she also holds that it must be taken to mean that we have responsibilities for each other and so we are priests *to* each other, not just our own priests.[140] Felton holds that baptism, a sacrament of equality, is the ordination into this priesthood.[141] A specialized priesthood is derived from this general priesthood and has as its function the service of the community of faith.[142] While her own tradition has a process for helping those who are considering professional ministry to discern their call, Felton contends that *all* Christians should be assisted in finding their calling.[143]

The charismatic nature of the church is part of the basis for Howard Snyder's push for renewing the church.[144] He chastises the church, saying "the contemporary church does not believe profoundly in the biblical doctrine of the gifts of the Spirit."[145] He makes a direct connection between the gifts of the Spirit and the priesthood of all believers. From 1 Peter 2:4–9, Snyder draws three implications: 1) we all have direct access to God, 2) we are priests to each other, and 3) this universal priesthood is for carrying out God's mission in the world, not just in the church.[146] Snyder observes that the priesthood of all believers has most often been understood soteriologically rather that ecclesiologically.[147] The soteriological framework emphasizes the direct access that each individual has to God. If the doctrine is framed in a way that includes an ecclesiological dimension, Snyder believes that the whole people of God are given the ministry of the church.

The Pentecostal theologian and ecumenist, Veli-Matti Kärkkäinen, points out that all Christian traditions today agree that the whole people

---

139. Felton, "A Royal Priesthood in a New Millennium," 373–74.

140. Ibid., 373–74.

141. Ibid., 373, 374, 379.

142. Ibid., 370.

143. Ibid., 374.

144. Snyder, *Liberating the Church*, 17, 89.

145. Ibid., 175.

146. Ibid., 172.

147. Ibid., 169.

of God is crucial in fulfilling God's mission in the world.[148] Kärkkäinen wants to push churches in all traditions to better reflect this conviction in their praxis. He believes that ecumenical progress can be made theologically and in praxis by emphasizing the charismatic or pneumatological structure of the church, an emphasis seen above in Snyder. This understanding of how the church is structured finds broad consensus, but this consensus does not carry over into understandings of ministry.[149] In order to make progress here, Kärkkäinen argues that the ministry of the Holy Spirit must be seen as broader than the ministries of word and sacrament.[150] This opens wide the door for the laity to participate in a meaningful way in the ministry of the church. Through an understanding that the Spirit ministers to the world through *all* Christians, not just through clergy, we can surmount the dichotomy between clergy and laity because "spiritual activity and receptiveness are no longer divided into two groups of persons, but represent two basic activities of each individual: each individual acts in the person of Christ and each is a recipient of this action."[151]

The New Reformation is the bold title Greg Ogden first gave to his book on the priesthood of all believers, now republished as *Unfinished Business: Returning the Ministry to the People of God.* Ogden's work has proven to be significant in Free church discussions even though Ogden writes from a Presbyterian background. Like Snyder and others, Ogden points to a growing awareness of the role of the Holy Spirit and gives this as a reason that the priesthood of all believers is at a point of recovery.[152] He works to erase the differing status between the clergy and the laity, and in fact proposes that we would be well served by eliminating the words "clergy" and "laity" from our ecclesial vocabulary.[153] He sets forth a model of the pastor as an equipper and argues that this model works toward, rather than against, the priesthood of all believers.[154] He calls for baptism to be recognized as ordination,[155] but he also allows for the rite of ordi-

---

148. Kärkkäinen, "The Calling of the Whole People of God into Ministry," 144.

149. Ibid., 152.

150. Ibid., 153. See also Kärkkäinen, "Church as Charismatic Fellowship," 100–121.

151. Kärkkäinen, "The Calling of the Whole People of God into Ministry," 154.

152. Ogden, *Unfinished Business*, 20.

153. Ibid., 96.

154. Ibid., 130–56.

155. Ibid., 267.

nation to a "special" ministry.[156] His overarching concern is to replace a dual-level status system in the church with a framework that includes only one status. In the end, though, he does not completely erase the line between clergy and laity. As a result, he weakens his own push for a single status within the church.

These voices show that the doctrine of the priesthood of all believers remains a topic of keen interest within the Free Church tradition. Unfortunately, some writers have allowed the institution of individualism[157] to infiltrate and distort the NT and historic Free Church understandings of the priesthood of all believers. Yet many voices within this tradition continue to rightly point out that *all* Christians are competent to come directly to God, that *all* Christians are called to ministry, that ecclesial leadership *is* accountable to the royal priesthood, and that this priesthood always has a corporate dimension.

I will now examine more closely the views of John Howard Yoder and Miroslav Volf. In different ways, both Yoder and Volf contribute to what I hold to be a theologically valid, Free Church approach to the priesthood of the whole people of God.

John Howard Yoder

In his book *The Fullness of Christ: Paul's Vision of Universal Ministry*, Mennonite theologian John Howard Yoder argues that the apostolic vision is that all believers are involved in ministry. This is a radical alternative to the anthropological norm of the religious specialist. All cultures create a place for the religious specialist, claims Yoder. On the surface, these specialists might look quite different, but they all share some basic characteristics. The religious specialist must be qualified (e.g., by birth, by education, or by some other form of selection), the specialist has certain functions that only he/she can carry out, the specialist's presence is seen as solemnizing an event, the specialist is remunerated in some way for his/her services, and the specialist does the things required to keep the religious institution going. [158] Yoder's thesis is that the apostolic vision of ministry must be understood as a rejection of all these anthropological

---

156. Ibid., 269.

157. This is one of several institutions I deal with in ch. 4.

158. Yoder, *The Fullness of Christ*, 1–5.

constants. The apostolic vision "represents not a refinement of, or a development from, but a radical alternative to this general religious model."[159]

Yoder looks at various terms in the NT that refer to leadership positions and concludes, as I did above, that ministry patterns in the NT reflect a great diversity. This conclusion regarding diversity is an important foundation of his argument. Having identified the diverse nature of ministry in the NT, Yoder goes on to ask an important theological question: is this diversity a historical accident?[160] He stresses that this pattern, rather than being accidental, is in fact a theological imperative. Yoder sets forth three aspects of this imperative. First, a diversity of ministry is to exist. This stems from the fact that many different functions are included in the varied lists of charisms found in the NT. Second, the ministries are to be plural. This claim derives from the observation that the biblical witness shows several people sharing in any given office. Third, ministry is to be universal. Every believer has a gift from the Holy Spirit that is to be used for building up the body of Christ. The giving of these gifts is part of the saving work of Christ (Eph. 4:8, Heb 2:4).[161] The priestly role that was firmly established in Judaism was not carried over by the early church. It was abolished.

While the multiplicity of ministries is a theological imperative, Yoder observes, "the weight of the anthropological constant, the 'drag of the race', soon succeeded in grinding down the originality, the charismatic universality of the first age."[162] The changes did not come suddenly, but rather took place in incremental ways. The result was a set of forms and functions that closely resembled the cultural norms rather than the original apostolic vision.[163] The multiplicity of ministries was lost.

---

159. Ibid., 6. In n. 1 above, I referred to the hermeneutical task as set forth by Richard Hays. In review, when undertaking the hermeneutical task we need to look for rules, principles, paradigms, and symbolic worlds. All of these are found in scriptures. Each must be handled according to its type. The fourth category, symbolic worlds, is at issue here in Yoder's work. By showing how the role of religious specialist is radically altered by the apostolic vision, Yoder is pointing to a fundamental shift in the symbolic world of the early Christians. This was not just a modification to a rule or principle within the existing symbolic world, but an alteration to the symbolic world itself.

160. Ibid., 14.

161. Ibid., 14–15.

162. Ibid., 17.

163. Ibid., 19.

One of Yoder's strengths is that he understands and anticipates the rebuttals of those who would challenge his assertions. He takes on two such challenges to his assertion regarding the apostolic vision of ministry. One challenge claims that an evolutionary process took place, a process already evident in the NT writings. Some would say that this was a process guided by the Holy Spirit, while others would say that it was a process guided by historical necessity.[164] Yoder takes on this challenge by looking at the NT texts used to support this view. He argues the conclusions reached by his challengers are a result of the preconceived notions of structure that these challengers bring to the texts. He puts forth alternative interpretations of the texts, interpretations he believes better represent what was really going on in the early churches.[165] In the end he concludes from examining these texts that the claimed evolutionary process does *not* find early manifestation in the NT.

A second challenge comes from those who would distinguish between gifts and office by claiming that gifts and office correlate to two different types of ministries. Yoder rebuts this challenge by examining the ways these two categories are differentiated. Some differentiate these categories on the basis of ordination. Others say that an office is given and taken away by a congregation while a gift does not need to be ratified by the congregation. Still others differentiate based on whether or not a function is related to church governance (e.g., bishops and elders govern, tongues and prophecy are not related to governance). Yoder methodically considers each of these and concludes that none are adequate for differentiating between gifts and office.[166]

One common way of distinguishing between office and charisms is based on a distorted view of charisms. Some have argued, says Yoder, that while office is permanent and stable, charisms are fluid and unpredictable.[167] This view is influenced by two modern usages of the term "charismatic," both of which obscure the NT meaning of this word. The term has developed a secular sense that a person has a certain emotional, personal appeal. Many Christians have also used it, especially since the 1960s, to refer to a particular set of spiritual gifts that includes speaking in tongues,

164. Ibid., 23–27.

165. I refer the interested reader to Yoder's book itself for the substance of these alternative explanations. See Ibid., 25–27.

166. Ibid., 28–30.

167. Ibid., 30.

prophecy, and healing.[168] Neither of these uses is helpful in seeking to understand the NT usage.

In order to help us more clearly understand what Paul means by "charismatic," Yoder points out that Paul is aware of and uses the Hellenistic word for spiritual gifts, *pneumatika*, but in most places Paul uses the word *charismata* instead. Paul gives this word a meaning distinct from the Hellenistic usage of *pneumatika*. Paul's meaning is distinct in three ways. First, Paul extends the concept beyond that of *pneumatika* to include even non-ecstatic gifts. Second, Paul asserts that these gifts are orderly and he rejects the unaccountable use of them, the self-justifying ecstatic utterances of paganism. Third, by changing to *charismata*, Paul emphasizes that these are "grace gifts," given by and dependant on the grace of God.[169]

Yoder states that these aspects would have been offensive to those Corinthians who thought of themselves as more spiritual because they had certain gifts, and Yoder finds it "ironic that a usage [of *charisma*] which Paul introduced in order thus to teach against over-valuing the special endowment of a few has come in modern usage to be a standard label for just what he was opposing."[170]

Throughout church history, Yoder observes, various groups have sought to renew the apostolic vision of ministry.[171] He gives especially helpful attention to the ecumenical discussions beginning in the 1950s. He argues that while these discussions have focused on the various forms of ministry and have highlighted the role of the laity, these discussions still operate on the assumption that "the ministry" is something carried out by a select few.[172] The arguments mainly involve a shift in emphasis

---

168. Ibid., 30, 32.

169. Ibid., 32–33.

170. Ibid., 33.

171. Ibid., 37–44.

172. Ibid., 45. Yoder makes the sharp observation that sometimes the language used in these ecumenical discussions is bold, such as when baptism is spoken of as ordination, but "yet the *substance* of what it now means for these laymen to be ministers seldom seems to go beyond the Reformation vision…of the service rendered to Christ in the world by means of one's gainful occupation" (46). The Eastern Orthodox ecclesiologist, John Zizioulas, is one who argues for baptism as ordination. Or to put it more accurately, he argues that baptism is *an* ordination. All Christians, by virtue of their baptism are ordained, but they are not ordained in the same way that ordained ministers are ordained. See Zizioulas, *Being as Communion*, 216. While he cannot be accused of holding "the

while maintaining the categories of laity and clergy.[173] Yoder proposes that ministry should be defined in terms of specific tasks, not in terms of which general group carries out these tasks. This approach, he contends, holds onto the idea of specialized ministry, but by giving these specialized ministries to the whole people of God, this approach does away with the idea of an undifferentiated laity.[174]

Proclamation has been viewed as one of these specialized tasks, and as a specialized task it has been used to distinguish the charism of office from other charisms. While acknowledging the importance of proclamation, Yoder provides an extended discussion of proclamation, which shows it to be not a specialized task, but a general task that can be carried out through the use of various specialized gifts. Nowhere in the NT, Yoder argues, is the task of proclamation reserved for a specialized clergy class.[175]

Yoder asserts that the renewal of the apostolic vision of ministry requires the recovery of an understanding of servanthood. This was part of the definition of Jesus's ministry and was to be the model for his disciples. This concept of the greatest being a servant is at once paradoxical and powerful, and "that is why one of Satan's most ordinary tricks is to let us continue to use the language of serving as a euphemism for ruling."[176]

In his quest to reclaim the apostolic vision of universal ministry, Yoder gives an extensive evaluation of the professionalism of ministry. He describes both positive and negative aspects of this professionalism and he rejects the temptation to rule in favor or against this process. Rather, he calls for a contextual evaluation of the professional ministry.[177] While he does not reject the professional ministry as such, he *does* reject certain aspects of it. While professionalism in most fields implies specialization, Yoder points out that the professional minister is in fact a generalist, a jack-of-all-trades, and Yoder argues that this does not fit with the NT view where we see the responsibilities "widely shared among numerous

---

Reformation vision" to which Yoder refers, it would seem that Zizioulas is guilty of the charges leveled by Yoder: using bold language regarding baptism as ordination, but in fact not changing the *substance* of what it means for all to be ordained.

173. Yoder, *The Fullness of Christ*, 46.

174. Ibid.

175. Ibid., 66.

176. Ibid., 67.

177. Ibid., 72–73.

persons, perhaps each of them less competent to do the whole job, but each of them probably more competent to do his or her one share than the average recent seminary graduate would be to handle everything."[178] Yoder also argues that the definition of profession includes the idea of ideological neutrality. For example, we would expect a brain surgeon to carry out his or her duties in a manner that is independent of his or her religious or political convictions. However, ministers must not take up this aspect of professionalism; those who minister in the name of Christ cannot avoid being theologically partisan.[179] Professionalism also implies interchangeability, but such a view taken into the church would fail to account for a person's unique personality and giftedness.[180] Interchangeability leads to mobility that is incompatible with many NT models of ministry.[181] The NT does set forth an itinerant role, but the central functions of local congregations were not handed over to these mobile ministers.[182] A final characteristic of professionalism is that it calls forth a level of excellence which cannot be expected of amateurs.[183] Yoder argues that this is clearly inconsistent with the Pauline concept of ministry, a concept that spreads responsibility among all the people rather than collecting it into the central role of a professional religionist.[184]

In the end, what are we to do? Should we try to go back to how things were done in the NT—a restorationist option? Or should we embrace the historical changes as legitimate? Yoder examines and rejects both options.[185] He does not seek to renew the NT pattern of church because

178. Ibid., 74.

179. Ibid., 77.

180. Ibid., 78.

181. 1 Tim 3 and Titus 1 set forth qualifications for leaders; for a community to know whether or not a person possesses these qualifications requires that the community know the person. Mobility prevents this type of knowledge. Ibid., 78–79.

182. Ibid., 79.

183. Ibid.

184. Yoder brings Paul's view into focus by saying, "the point in the Pauline multiple ministry notion is not that by the division of labor more can get done, nor that there is too much for one man to do, nor that people are more likely to support an organization which needs them, nor that democracy has taught the laity to want a voice in their government. All these things might be true, but they are not the main points. Paul's point is that each task can be better done by its own bearer. The stomach cannot do the eye's work; the ear is not merely a defective nose or an amateur nose; it is no nose at all." Ibid.

185. Ibid., 86–90.

no single normative pattern can be found. At the same time, he rejects changes which are embraced uncritically, particularly the development of the mono-pastoral pattern. What, then, can be the basis for evaluating congregational structures and practices? Yoder argues that, while no single pattern can be found in the NT, commonalities exist between the various patterns, commonalities that were intentional, not accidental.[186] While great flexibility existed, constants within this flexibility include plural leadership as opposed to a mono-pastoral pattern, diversity of roles, universality of ministry, the need for local congregational leadership, a teaching function, itineration, and prophets communicating on behalf of the Holy Spirit.[187] These constants still allow for change, and Yoder sets forth several tools for *responsible* change, change that is consistent with these NT constants of ministry.[188]

As he wraps up his arguments against the religious specialist and for the apostolic vision of ministry shared by all believers, Yoder makes a final plea for universal ministry:

> Even if the shared ministry were not more effective, or in line with the newest thinking on leadership techniques, or a safeguard against certain pitfalls—all of which it is—it would still be desirable by virtue of the calling of each to exercise his or her own "come-of-ageness," by the imperative of spiritual responsibility.[189]

In an exegetically solid and theologically convincing manner, Yoder challenges the development of the religious specialist. He argues that while no single NT pattern of ministry exists, the patterns that we see in the NT have several things in common. One commonality is the rejection of the role of religious specialist. Another commonality is that the various NT models recognize that all the people of God have charisms and all charisms are to be used for ministry. In my view, Yoder makes an important contribution to the discussion of the priesthood of all believers, a contribution that is sound biblically and theologically.

---

186. Ibid., 90.

187. Ibid., 91.

188. Ibid. Yoder explicitly states that he is not trying to set forth a full model of ministry for today. No single model exists and all viable models must be contextual.

189. Ibid., 104.

Miroslav Volf

In *After Our Likeness: The Church as the Image of the Trinity*, Miroslav Volf sets forth a compelling ecclesiology and does significant work to show how the whole people of God is related to the nature and structures of the church. In order to provide greater clarity regarding how Volf relates the church to the universal priesthood, I will first describe how this part of his discussion fits into the broader organization of his argument. Volf claims that any discussion of the *structure* of the church must be preceded by a discussion of the *nature* of the church. The latter must shape the former. Volf discusses the nature of the church by examining the ecclesiality of the church (chpt. III), the relationship of the church to the mediation of salvation (chpt. IV), and the correspondences between the Trinity and the church (chpt. V). He contends that it is only in light of these discussions that we can then credibly carry out an examination of church structures. Volf's examination of church structures has three basic parts. He looks at participation and charismata, the Trinity and ecclesial institutions, and ordination.

Volf points out that Catholic and Orthodox Church structures are episcopocentric.[190] In both ecclesiologies the bishop alone acts *in persona Christi*.[191] Volf rejects an episcopocentric model of the church based on his contention:

> (1) that the church is not a single subject, but rather a communion of interdependent subjects, (2) that the mediation of salvation occurs not only through office-holders, but also through all other members of the church, and (3) that the church is constituted by the Holy Spirit not so much by way of the institution of office as through the communal confession in which Christians speak the word of God to one another.[192]

Because of these convictions, Volf argues that the church is constituted by the participation of the whole people of God. This leads him to promote a *polycentric* rather than episcopocentric ecclesial model.[193] He supports his argument for a polycentric model by pointing to the fact that each Christian receives a general call to ministry when he/she enters into the

190. Volf, *After Our Likeness*, 223.

191. Ibid., 223–24.

192. Ibid., 224.

193. Ibid.

faith.[194] He also supports it by pointing out that each Christian is given one or more specific charisms which are empowerments from God for carrying out God's mission in the world.[195] Volf observes that this polycentric participative model of community simply describes what has actually been going on all along: the mediation of faith by a whole range of people, not just office holders.[196] He also claims that the episcopocentric view has contributed to the passivity of the laity, and he sees this polycentric model as working against such passivity.[197]

Volf places great importance on the charisms because he holds that Christ himself is at work through these gifts.[198] He describes several characteristics of the charisms. First, the charisms are always confessional in nature, whether explicitly or implicitly.[199] Christ is present in the charisms, and so every use of them confesses Christ as Lord and Savior. Second, the Holy Spirit gives every Christian at least one charism, that is, the charisms are universally distributed.[200] Third, the charisms are characterized by their mutual interdependence.[201] They are not to function in isolation. It is when they are used in conjunction with the other gifts in the body of Christ that they find their full expression. Fourth, the Holy Spirit distributes the charisms.[202] Volf provides an insightful discussion of how the Spirit distributes these charisms. While the Spirit gives them, we are instructed to strive for them (1 Cor 12:31; 14:1). This striving is to be done in light of one's self-knowledge and in light of the confirmation of this knowledge by the community. Thus Volf asserts that the Spirit distributes charisms by means of an interactional model. Fifth, Volf argues that the charisms are both diachronic and synchronic. By "synchronic" he means that a person can have more than one gift at a time. By "diachronic" he means that charisms are not permanent and can change over time.[203]

194. Ibid., 225.

195. Ibid., 226.

196. Ibid., 227.

197. Ibid. Volf acknowledges that other factors also contribute to lay passivity, but this theological elevation of the laity is an important first step in overcoming it (228).

198. Ibid., 228.

199. Ibid., 229.

200. Ibid., 229–30.

201. Ibid., 231.

202. Ibid., 231–33.

203. Ibid., 233.

In addition to the charisms, Volf makes the nature of the Trinity important for a discussion of the priesthood of all believers. He rejects Ratzinger's view of the Trinity as monocentric and he rejects Zizioulas's view of the Trinity as hierarchic.[204] Volf holds that the relations within the Trinity are symmetrical. Based on this, he posits the ecclesial principle that "the more a church is characterized by symmetrical and decentralized distribution of power and freely affirmed interaction, the more will it correspond to the trinitarian communion."[205] Such a view is a strong affirmation of the importance to the church of the whole people of God.

In Volf's view, a church can be a church without officeholders. He does not tie office to the *esse* of the church. At the same time, for a church to endure, he believes it does need to have officeholders, either formally or informally. So while they do not belong to the *esse* of the church, officeholders are needed for the ongoing life of the community.[206]

What is the nature of ordination, the rite used to install officeholders? Volf rejects both the Free church view that ordination is the delegation of office by the congregation and the episcopal view that ordination marks the deliverance of the charism of office through the act of a bishop.[207] Instead, he claims that "ordination is to be understood as a public reception of a charisma given by God and focused on the local church as a whole."[208] Ordination is also "an act of the entire local church led by the Spirit of God."[209] The Holy Spirit gives the charism, but it is not activated for use in the life of the church until the entire local church receives it. Thus Volf views ordination not just as a divine event nor just as a human event, but as a divine-human event.[210]

Volf argues that the charism of office, like every other charism, is not necessarily given for life, although it might be. He points out that in the NT, the laying on of hands (which Volf equates with ordination) is always tied to a specific task. So, Volf contends, when a person is given a

---

204. Ibid., 236.

205. Ibid.

206. Ibid., 248.

207. Ibid., 248–49.

208. Ibid., 249.

209. Ibid.

210. Ibid.

new task, a new ordination is appropriate. Ordination, unlike baptism, is a repeatable event.[211]

Much of Volf's argument regarding ordination works to close the gap between the ministerial priesthood and the common priesthood. All believers have charisms, and office is just one of the many charisms distributed by the Spirit. The contingent nature of office is something the charism of office shares with all others. Just as the Spirit freely gives charisms—including the charism of office, the Spirit is also free to take away and replace charisms. Yet in Volf's view, a difference remains between the charism of office and all other charisms. According to Volf, the charism of office, unlike all the other charisms, is referenced to the entirety of the local church.

I find this view problematic for several reasons. First, can we rightly join our Catholic brothers and sisters in speaking of "a charism of office"? Might not a *variety* of charisms qualify one for office? I suggest that charisms are *related* to office, but must not be *equated* with office. Second, while Volf sees his approach as overcoming the divide between the ministerial and common priesthoods, does he not in fact leave intact the distinction between these two priesthoods, theologically and sociologically, because he continues to distinguish between the charism of office and all the other charisms? Third, are we justified in distinguishing between charisms that are referenced to the entirety of the local congregation and those that are not? In chapter three I will offer a different view of charisms that addresses these issues.

My disagreements with Volf are minor in comparison to my overall embrace of his ecclesiological project. By first discussing the ecclesiality of the church, the ways in which salvation is mediated, and trinitarian correspondence, Volf constructs a solid theological foundation that has been lacking in many Free church discussions of the priesthood of all believers. He makes a significant contribution to the Free church tradition and at the same time he interacts with voices from outside this tradition, thus contributing to the broader ecumenical discussion as well.

---

211. Ibid., 251.

CONCLUSION

I contend that the eschatological vision for the people of God is one in which a single priesthood, a priesthood composed of all believers, exists. All Christians are priests and are called into the ministerial service of God. The NT witness indicates that the early church did not carry forward Jewish understandings of the priesthood as a select subset of people. Rather, priesthood was re-conceived as an all-inclusive social order, one in which all believers participate. This original vision became distorted as the church developed. A priestly class was re-established, and for much of the history of the church both a common and a ministerial priesthood have existed. The existence of these two priesthoods has been both justified and critiqued as theological discussions regarding the nature of the priesthood of all believers have continued. Some Free church voices have wrongly sought to redefine the royal priesthood in individualistic terms, as reflected in their use of the phrase "the priesthood of the believer." In contrast, the works of Yoder and Volf point to the corporate nature of this priesthood. Yoder is on target when he claims that Christianity is revolutionary in its rejection of the religious specialist, a rejection that comes from the egalitarian impulses of the apostolic vision. Volf rightly argues for a view of the church that is polycentric, a view that emerges from his understanding that all believers are gifted for ministry. In the next chapter, as I work to ground the royal priesthood in a trinitarian ecclesiology, I do so with an awareness that I stand in the long shadows of these voices, both past and present, who have also taken up the cause of the royal priesthood.

THREE

An Ecclesiology that Demands a Royal Priesthood

The nature of the royal priesthood is directly related to the relationship between the Trinity and the church. In this chapter I set forth an ecclesiology that is grounded in a relational understanding of the Trinity. I then point to specific characteristics that must define the royal priesthood in light of this ecclesiology. I show how the nature of the charisms plays a significant role in connecting the Trinity, the church, and the royal priesthood. Finally, I argue that ordination must be reconceptualized in a manner that is consistent with this theology of the royal priesthood.

Trinitarian considerations are vital in ecclesiological reflections, yet these are not the *only* issues that are relevant. The scriptural narratives, eschatological perspectives, and social and ecclesial experience must also be considered. While my focus here is on the trinitarian connections, these other voices must not be forgotten and at points in the discussion I shall draw these in as well.

THE JUSTIFICATION OF A TRINITARIAN ECCLESIOLOGY

Locating the Argument

Kant believed "nothing whatsoever can be gathered for practical purposes" from the doctrine of the Trinity.[1] On the other hand, Nicholas Fedorov argued "the dogma of the Trinity is our social program."[2] Given the extreme range of views as represented by Kant and Fedorov, we must

1. Moltmann, *The Trinity and the Kingdom*, 62.
2. Volf, "'The Trinity Is Our Social Program,'" 403.

consider the validity of arguing for connections between the Trinity and social/ecclesial structures. Are we justified in expecting the church to mirror and participate in the Trinity? What limits, if any, might be required for such a project? Miroslav Volf has given constructive attention to these questions, and I turn now to an examination of his approach.

According to Volf, Fedorov believed that Christians possess full power to regulate and shape society.[3] Fedorov based this contention on his belief that Christians already fully participate in the eschatological promise of God. Believers and the social structures they promote can and should copy God in all respects. Volf rejects this extreme realized eschatology, but he accepts the basic proposal that correspondence exists between the Trinity and social/ecclesial constructs.

At the opposite extreme from Fedorov, Volf places Ted Peters. Peters rejects the project of shaping society based on the Trinity. He argues against this project because he asserts that we must understand God and humans disjunctively, not conjunctively.[4] Peters states, "the image of the immanent Trinity ought not be used as a model for human society"[5] because "we as creatures cannot copy God in all respects."[6] The problem is that Peters ignores the possibility that we can copy God in *some* respects.

Volf argues for an alternative to the positions of Fedorov and Peters, an alternative that incorporates elements of each. Volf's rhetoric is powerful as he argues that Christians can indeed speak of correspondence between the Trinity and the social order:

> . . . would it not be odd to claim there are no analogues to God in creation and yet to maintain, as Christian theologians must, that human beings are made in the image of God? And would it not be anomalous to insist that human beings, created for communion

---

3. Ibid., 403, 404.

4. Peters, *God as Trinity*, 186. It is worth noting that Peters in some respects ends up in the same place as many social trinitarians—arguing against injustice and for egalitarian communities—but he arrives there based on the eschatological kingdom of God, not based on the nature of the Trinity (186). In his treatment of Moltmann (103–110), Peters acknowledges the key role of eschatology in Moltmann's thought, but Peters does not carry this combination of Trinity and eschatology forward as an option. He chooses instead to opt for the eschatological kingdom—and rejects the Trinity—as the appropriate model for society. For an example of how Moltmann holds the two together, see Moltmann, *The Trinity and the Kingdom*, 95.

5. Peters, *God as Trinity*, 184.

6. Ibid., 186.

with the Triune . . . God and renewed through faith and baptism into the Triune name "according to the likeness of God" (Ephesians 4:24), should not seek to be like God in their mutual relations? If the idea of an image that is *not* supposed to reflect the reality of which it is an image does not strike us as odd, Jesus' injunction in the Sermon on the Mount should set us straight: "Be perfect," he commands his disciples, "as your heavenly Father is perfect" (Matthew 5:48; cf. 1 Peter 1:16). The earthly children should be like their heavenly parent, he states (v. 45); the character of God should shape the character and behavior of those who worship, he implies.[7]

Should the children of the triune God—and the church as their primary social structure—reflect the Trinity? Yes! In his argument *against* this, Peters seems to ignore the fact that we are created in the image of God, a fact that must result in trinitarian correspondence as Volf has argued. Because we are created in the image of a triune God, who we are—including our relationships and social structures—must to some degree reflect the Trinity. The question, then, "is not whether the Trinity *should* serve as a model for human community; the question is rather *in which respects* and *to what extent* it should do so."[8] I shall look now at how Volf takes up the challenge of elucidating these parameters.

Limits

While Volf agrees with Fedorov's basic idea that the Trinity provides a model for society, Volf departs from Fedorov by asserting that we cannot copy the Trinity in all respects. As we search of correspondence between the Trinity and the church, we must do so within certain bounds. Volf sets forth three basic limits. First, like Peters, we must assert that a disjunction

7. Volf, "'The Trinity Is Our Social Program,'" 404.

8. Ibid., 405 (my emphasis). Working out an answer to this question is by no means an easy feat as we can see by the fact that Leonardo Boff and Michael Novak both tie their social programs to the nature of the Trinity but end up advocating (a form of) socialism and democratic capitalism respectively. Interestingly, their disagreement does not center on the nature of the Trinity—both build on relational trinitarianism and both insist that differentiation must be maintained within the Trinity and within society. It is on the question of how to best reflect the trinitarian nature that they diverge dramatically. See Boff, *Trinity and Society*, 148–52; and Novak, *The Spirit of Democratic Capitalism*, 338–40. My task here is somewhat different in that I am not seeking to develop a model for society as a whole, but rather, a vision for the church.

exists between God and humans (though in contrast to Peters, Volf argues that this disjunction is not absolute). Only God is God. Humans are not God and therefore cannot mirror God in every way. As created beings, we are to correspond to God in creaturely ways.[9] Our correspondence to God is circumscribed by our humanness. The second limit is also anthropological in nature: all trinitarian models, like language, reveal God anthropomorphically. We must acknowledge that no trinitarian model can fully capture the mystery of the triune God. In part, God remains hidden and so our imitations of God can only be partial.[10] Third, our correspondence is conditioned by the eschatological horizon which we have not yet reached (in contrast to Fedorov's fully realized eschatology). The church's trinitarian correspondence must be understood dynamically because the church is on a journey from the historical to the eschatological.[11] The church's trinitarian correspondence must be historically grounded but not static. Only in the fullness of the eschaton will the church reach the fullness of its trinitarian correspondence.

A danger in this project is that we can easily create an image of the Trinity that justifies the views we already hold regarding the nature of the church. Volf rightly points out that egalitarian constructions of the Trinity can appear to be

> projections onto God of the shallow democratic sentiments which emerged when modern, functionally-differentiated societies replaced traditional, hierarchically-segmented societies. The denials of hierarchy in the Trinity, so the argument, seem to be fueled more by the falsely egalitarian spirit of the age than shaped by the revelation of the character of God.[12]

But what if the Trinity *does* in fact produce an egalitarian impulse? Are we to deny this impulse because it already exists in the current cultural context? The danger can never be overcome, but this does not mean we should then say nothing. Following the lead of Volf and others, I acknowledge the danger but choose nonetheless to venture forward in this

---

9. Volf, "'The Trinity Is Our Social Program,'" 405. Also, Volf, *After Our Likeness*, 199.

10. Volf, *After Our Likeness*, 198.

11. Ibid., 199.

12. Volf, "'The Trinity Is Our Social Program,'" 407. Ted Peters goes further, arguing that this is not just a danger, but that this is in fact what has happened. See Peters, *God as Trinity*, 185.

direction because of its rich potential for informing the church's identity and shaping the church's life.

To summarize, we are justified to look for correspondence between the Trinity and the church, but we must do so with an awareness of the limits of such correspondence. The church's correspondence is constrained by both our limited knowledge of God and our historically located human imperfections. We must be careful not to simply construct a Trinity in order to justify what we already embrace. With these points in mind, I shall proceed with my exploration of the nature of the Trinity and how this might shape ecclesiology.

RELATIONAL TRINITARIANISM

The theology of the royal priesthood that I am developing emerges from an ecclesiology tied to a relational view of the Trinity, and so I begin by expounding on this approach to trinitarianism. As Stanley Grenz has noted, trinitarian theology today is dominated by relational approaches. He asserts that by the end of the twentieth century "the assumption that the most promising beginning point for a viable trinitarian theology lies in the constellation of relationships among the three trinitarian persons had become so widely accepted that it attained a kind of quasi-orthodox status."[13] Relational approaches to the Trinity are pluriform. I suggest that enough commonality exists, however, to allow for my constructive ecclesiological work to proceed without resolving all the trinitarian issues that continue to be debated. I will show how the commonality in several differing understandings of the relational Trinity can be drawn upon to speak about the trinitarian nature of the church.

Jürgen Moltmann sets forth one such approach that emphasizes the relationality of the Trinity. He refers to his view as a "social doctrine of the Trinity."[14] Moltmann argues that an adequate understanding of the Trinity must give prominence to the Persons within the Trinity in order to avoid strict monotheism that precludes trinitarianism. Each Person in the Trinity must be seen as unique. Each has a divine nature that is not

13. Grenz, *Rediscovering the Triune God*, 117–18. I will refer to the three parts of the Trinity as "persons" but I will not enter into the discussion of what is meant by "persons." To access this discussion, see Moltmann, *The Trinity and the Kingdom*, 171–74; and Zizioulas, *Being as Communion*, 27–49, passim.

14. Moltmann, *The Trinity and the Kingdom*, viii.

identical with the others. This means that differentiation exists within the Trinity.[15] Mutual indwelling—perichoresis—characterizes the nature of the Trinity, and for Moltmann this serves as the basis for trinitarian unity.[16] The differentiation within the Trinity is bound together into a unity because the three Persons always exist perichoretically. Their identities are tied to the inter-trinitarian relationships, though this is not to say that the Persons *are* relationships.

Moltmann's social trinitarianism has been criticized as tritheistic, and although Moltmann himself vehemently denies this,[17] his approach does raise concern. Ted Peters states flatly that Moltmann is no polytheist,[18] but he goes on to assert that Moltmann's "continued emphasis on three discrete subjects or centers of activity makes it difficult to conceive of a principle of unity that is comparable to that of the plurality."[19] Regardless of whether or not we can go all the way with Moltmann, his approach does give credibility to a relational understanding of the Trinity.

Wolfhart Pannenberg also focuses on the relational nature of the Trinity.[20] Pannenberg grounds his doctrine of the Trinity in history: it is on the basis of the historical revelation of the three—Father, Son, and Spirit—that we are then moved to ask about their oneness or unity. As a result, Pannenberg sees trinitarian relations rather than the one divine substance as the place to begin in drawing out the nature of the Trinity.[21]

The importance for Pannenberg of the relationships in the Trinity can be seen in his understanding of how the three members of the Trinity receive their divinity. In his view, the divinity of the three members is not something that each member has independently of the others. Each member is divine because this divinity is given by the others. It is a *dependent* divinity. Peters notes that in Pannenberg's thinking the divinity of each member of the Trinity "comes to each as the result of the personhood of relationship."[22] Pannenberg summarizes this position by stating that "in their intratrinitarian relations the persons depend on one another in

15. Ibid., 172.

16. Ibid., 175.

17. Ibid.

18. Peters, *God as Trinity*, 109.

19. Ibid.

20. See especially Pannenberg, *Systematic Theology*, 308–319.

21. Peters, *God as Trinity*, 136.

22. Ibid., 138.

respect of their deity."[23] The trinitarian relations are the means by which divinity is granted and received within the Godhead.

The idea of perichoresis comes out in Pannenberg's work. Although he does not accept Moltmann's move of using perichoresis as the fundamental basis for trinitarian unity,[24] Pannenberg affirms the reciprocity of relationships contained in the concept.[25] Mutual relationality is a key part of the trinitarian nature in Pannenberg's estimation.

The Orthodox theologian John Zizioulas reaches back to the Cappadocians in his work to describe the Trinity. Zizioulas asserts that *hypostasis* (concrete individuality) and *ousia* (what a thing *is*, one's essential nature) were understood synonymously by writers like Athanasius and his contemporaries. Zizioulas claims that the Cappadocians made a key move by dissociating *hypostasis* from *ousia* and linking *hypostasis* instead to *prosopon* (person).[26] This allowed for the affirmation of the ontological integrity of the threeness of God. Because relationships are required for personal identity, beings—whether created or divine—have personhood only through communion. The personal God is ontologically relational.[27]

Zizioulas further develops his relational understanding of the Trinity by building on the statement in Scripture that God is love (1 John 4:16). Zizioulas takes this as a basic ontological statement rather than a secondary quality. "God is love," in his view, "signifies that God 'subsists' as Trinity, that is, as person and not as substance."[28] Love is *constitutive* of God's substance. So "*to be* and *to be in relation* becomes identical."[29] Communion characterizes the nature of being—both divine and human.

We might summarize these views of the Trinity by saying that Moltmann emphasizes the plurality of persons, Pannenberg emphasizes the dependent nature of divinity, and Zizioulas emphasizes communion

---

23. Pannenberg, *Systematic Theology*, 329.

24. Ibid., 334.

25. Ibid., 319.

26. Zizioulas, *Being as Communion*, 87–88. Volf notes that Zizioulas's interpretation of the Cappadocians has been sharply criticized. See Volf, *After Our Likeness*, 75. What is of foremost importance to us is not whether his reading of the Cappadocians is accurate, but the view of the Trinity that Zizioulas himself promotes.

27. Zizioulas, *Being as Communion*, 88.

28. Ibid., 46.

29. Ibid., 88.

as the ground of being. They have in common the elevation of trinitarian relations in such a way that these relations are no longer secondary to substance in terms of the ontological nature of the Trinity. All three theologians hold that relationships replace substance as the most fruitful starting point for probing the mysteries of the Trinity.

Biblical Grounding

The relational nature of the Trinity is attested to in the Scriptures. While we do not have a developed trinitarianism in the Scriptures, we *are* given a number of insights into the relational nature of the Father, Son, and Spirit.

God is revealed in the OT to be the God of the Covenant with his people. Covenant requires relationship. This God wants to assimilate all people to himself (cf. Gen 9), and such assimilation is a relational move. The communion that God desires with Israel (cf. Exod 19, 24; Lev 26:11) is symbolic of the communion God desires with all peoples. As Boff notes, the relationship that God desires with his people is not just a political one, but also an interior one marked by intimacy (cf. Jer 31:33).[30]

In the NT we see clearly that the natures of the Father, Son, and Spirit are relational. An intimate relationship exists between the Father and the Son—no one knows the Son like the Father and vice versa (Matt 11:27). In fact, Jesus and the Father are one (John 10:30). John repeatedly uses the "being-in" language to express the relations between the Father and the Son and the communion of the Father and the Son with the people of God (cf. John 10:38; 14:11; 17:21–23). This relationship has existed from the beginning (John 1:1–2; Col. 1:15–17) At many points a relationship between Jesus and the Spirit is indicated, even if the exact nature of this relationship is not detailed (Luke 1:35; 3:22; 4:1; John 14:16–17, 26; 15:26; 16:7, 14). In addition to being in relationship with the Son, the Spirit is in relationship with people. The Spirit advocates on their behalf, abides with and in the people, and teaches and reminds the people about what Jesus said to them (John 14:16–17, 26). The Spirit is described in terms that show the Spirit's relational nature: believers are in the Spirit and the Spirit dwells in them (Rom 8:9, 11; 2 Tim 1:14). The Spirit reveals God to people

---

30. Boff, *Trinity and Society*, 131.

(1 Cor 2:10) and the Spirit bestows the gifts of God upon people (1 Cor 12:11; Heb 2:4). Based on the NT witness, Olson and Hall conclude:

> "Father," "Word," and "Wisdom" were not inconsequential characteristics of a paternal deity but rather a foretelling of a present and future relationship with God and his covenant people. Therefore we find that the God of salvation is not only one, but also three, unified in the inner relations of Father, Son, and Holy Spirit. The biblical God is Triune.[31]

As Olson and Hall point out, the characteristics of God point up God's relational nature. The God revealed in the scriptures as Father, Son, and Holy Spirit is relational.

Perichoresis

Pseudo-Cyril, writing in the sixth century, may have been the first one to apply the word "perichoresis" to the Trinity, though it was John of Damascus in the eighth century who lodged it permanently in trinitarian vocabulary.[32] Perichoresis refers to the mutual indwelling of the three Persons of the Trinity, or as Volf puts it, the "reciprocal *interiority*" of these three Persons.[33] The perichoretic nature of the Trinity means that the trinitarian Persons not only relate to each other, but actually indwell each other so as to possess the most intimate type of relationships possible. This indwelling is reciprocal. Each Person indwells and is indwelt by the other two Persons. This is what Jesus pointed to when he said, "the Father is in me and I am in the Father" (John 10:38; cf. 14:10–11; 17:21). Each Person of the Trinity permeates the others.[34]

---

31. Olson and Hall, *The Trinity*, 10.

32. Boff, *Trinity and Society*, 135; Fiddes, *Participating in God*, 71; Pannenberg, *Systematic Theology*, 319.

33. Volf, *After Our Likeness*, 209.

34. Boff and Fiddes both point out that two Latin words have been used to translate perichoresis from the Greek. The first, circuminsessio, refers to the way in which the Persons of the Trinity occupy the same space or are surrounded by one another. It has a static sense to it. The second, circumincessio, refers to the way in which the Persons relate to one another. This meaning is active and dynamic. It signifies the interweaving and interpenetration of the divine Persons. Boff, *Trinity and Society*, 134–36, Fiddes, *Participating in God*, 71–72. Perichoresis carries within it both senses, but it is the latter sense that is at the heart of relational trinitarianism.

Paul Fiddes sets forth a slightly different understanding of perichoresis. He sees value

Moltmann uses perichoresis to describe the way in which the three Persons are inextricably bound together into one.[35] This interpenetration means that the three Persons cannot be understood "as three different individuals, who only subsequently enter into relationship with one another."[36] Thus he argues that the unity within the Trinity is not achieved through one substance, but through the perichoretic relationships of the three.

At the same time, the uniqueness of each Person is not negated, a negation that would result in modalism. In fact, as Volf points out, distinct Persons are *required* for indwelling, for one cannot indwell oneself: "persons who have dissolved into one another cannot exist in one another."[37]

Perichoresis provides a way to understand the simultaneous uniqueness and oneness of the Trinity. The unifying relationships and the individual Persons exist at once. As Volf puts it, "personality and relationships are *genetically connected*, . . . the two arise simultaneously and together. The constitutions of the Persons and their manifestation through their relations are two sides of the same thing."[38] This brings us back to the basic

---

in the approach of Moltmann and his followers, but rather than conceiving of the Trinity as three Persons who have relations, Fiddes picks up the idea of subsistent relations and argues that the Trinity should be understood as "an event of relationships." (36) Stemming from this, he speaks of a perichoresis of relationships rather than a perichoresis of Persons. (83) Fiddes suggests that the metaphor which best captures the nature of the trinitarian relations is that of a dance, a divine dance in which "the partners not only encircle each other and weave in and out between each other as in human dancing: in the divine dance, so intimate is the communion that they move in and through each other so that the pattern is all inclusive." (72) He calls for a focus on the movements or relationships within the divine dance and eschews attempts to observe the persons on the ends of these relationships. (79) This is problematic, however, because not only can we not see the Persons on the ends of these relationships, Fiddes seems to hold that there *are* no Persons on the ends of these relationships. The distinctions for Fiddes between the Father, Son, and Holy Spirit seem to be not distinctions between Persons but between ways of relating or types of activity. If we focus solely on the movements of the dance as Fiddes suggests, how do we know that the dance is carried out by partners? Might not the dance movements, varied though they are, be carried out by a solitary figure dancing alone? While Moltmann may be in danger of tritheism, in my estimation Fiddes is in danger of modalism. See Fiddes, *Participating in God*.

35. Moltmann, *The Trinity and the Kingdom*, 175.

36. Ibid.

37. Volf, *After Our Likeness*, 209.

38. Moltmann, *The Trinity and the Kingdom*, 173.

premise of relational trinitarianism: relationships, rather than substance, need to be the starting point for discussing the triune nature.

If the Trinity is by nature relational, as I believe it is, then this has significant implications for our ecclesiology. I shall now set forth a number of ways in which a relational trinitarianism shapes the church.

A TRINITARIAN ECCLESIOLOGY:
CORRESPONDENCE AND PARTICIPATION

Insights into the nature of the Trinity inform our view of the church and its structures. In Volf's words, the Trinity is the "determining reality" of the church.[39] The ways in which the Trinity determines the nature of the church can be put into two general categories: correspondence and participation. In many ways the church is called to correspond to or mirror the Trinity. The church is also called to participate in the Trinity because the triune God has opened God's self up to such participation. As Moltmann puts it,

> Through the sending of the creative Spirit, the trinitarian history of God becomes a history that is open to the world, open to men and women, and open to the future. Through the experience of the life-giving Spirit in faith, in baptism, and in the fellowship of believers, people are integrated into the history of the Trinity. Through the Spirit of Christ they not only become participants in the eschatological history of the new creation, but through the Spirit of the Son they also become at the same time participants in the trinitarian history of God himself.[40]

The church does not determine the nature of God, but the church does participate in the life of God. The church is to model itself after the

---

39. Volf, *After Our Likeness*, 195.

40. Moltmann, *The Trinity and the Kingdom*, 90. Paul Fiddes buys into the social nature of the Trinity, but he argues that the type of perichoresis of persons that Moltmann and Boff advocate runs the risk of becoming a closed circle, a self-enclosed divine communion. See Fiddes, *Participating in God*, 78. Given the emphasis that Moltmann gives to the openness of God, Fiddes's charge is rather baffling. Moltmann argues that such self-enclosure would in fact violate the very nature of the Trinity: "the notion of an immanent Trinity in which God is simply by himself, without the love which communicates salvation, brings an arbitrary element into the concept of God which means a break-up of the Christian concept." (Moltmann, *The Trinity and the Kingdom*, 151). Moltmann does *not* have an understanding of the Trinity as self-enclosed.

Trinity even as the church participates in the Trinity. I shall now look at ways in which the Trinity shapes the nature of the church.

Relationality

The relationality of the Trinity, which characterizes the Trinity's existence, calls for a relational ecclesiology. This relationality is evident in Christ's teaching that where two or three are gathered in his name, he is there with them (Matt 18:30). Volf sees in these words the essence of the church.[41] The gathering of two or three is not in itself a church; to this must be added Christ's objective constitutive presence.[42] But without the gathering of believers—without the subjective act of at least two or three gathering together in Christ's name—the church does not exist. As the Trinity is constituted by relationships, so the church is constituted by relationships.[43]

If the trinitarian relations are perichoretic, it would seem to follow, then, that relations within the church should be perichoretic. But how can believers indwell each other? How can people live perichoretically? Volf rightly points out the limits of analogy here. A person cannot indwell another person in precisely the same way that the persons of the Trinity indwell each other. Another human cannot indwell me as a subject of action. I always remain the subject, the initiator of an action. Also, the way the divine Persons relate to me is different from the way they relate to each other within the Trinity because I cannot indwell the divine Persons in the same way that they indwell each other.[44]

However, there *is* a way set forth in Scripture in which we *do* indwell the Trinity. When Jesus said to his disciples, "on that day you will know that I am in my Father, and you in me, and I in you" (John 14:20), he pointed to the type of indwelling applicable to humans. It is the form of perichoresis available to humans who are limited by their creaturely

---

41. Volf, *After Our Likeness*, 135–36.

42. Ibid., 145.

43. This emphasis on relationality nudges the traditional marks of the church from center stage. The sacraments of word and table remain important, and in fact Volf argues that they continue to belong to the *esse* of the church, but they are conditions of ecclesiality "only if they are a form of the confession of faith and an expression of faith" (Ibid., 152–53).

44. Ibid., 211.

nature. The Holy Spirit is the agent of the ongoing work of Christ, and thus it is through the Holy Spirit that this indwelling occurs. Believers live perichoretically not by indwelling each other, but by relating perichoretically with and through Christ as represented by the Holy Spirit.

The correspondence here is also limited by human brokenness. Because of human sinfulness, we cannot exist in perfect relationships, as does the Trinity. Yet we are to be journeying from the historical minimum of our tarnished communion to the eschatological maximum of full trinitarian correspondence.[45]

Because the church should correspond to the Trinity, relationships are constitutive of the church. Relationships push out office as constitutive of the church. Volf states, "in whatever way "office" may indeed be desirable for church life, either in apostolic succession or not, it is *not necessary for ecclesiality*."[46] When office is extracted from the *esse* of the church, and when relationships are tied to the ecclesiality of the church, the priesthood of all believers becomes central because the gathering of *any* two or three Christians, even if none of them are office holders, constitutes the church.[47] The hierarchy and office holders, though they perhaps belong to the *benne esse* of the church, do not belong to its ecclesiality. Thus the importance of *all* believers is elevated.

If relationality is part of ecclesiality, I must assert the obvious: *people* are essential to the church. Though the church can properly be described as an institution, its institutional existence is dependent on the presence of believers gathered in Christ's name. The relationships between Christians are crucial to the existence of the church. And just as no relationship within the Trinity can be said to be more important than the others, in the church no relationships are more important than others. All persons and relationships within the church are ontologically equal.

Presence

The relational nature of the Trinity means that each Person of the Trinity is present with and for the others. Being present with another means as-

45. Ibid., 207.

46. Ibid., 152 (emphasis original).

47. I will not discuss here how the constitution of the local church relates to the constitution of the universal church. For a treatment of this important discussion, see Ibid., 200–204.

suming an inviting posture that hears and receives the other, and involves a movement toward the other. Presence is more than physical proximity. One can be present with another physically and yet not be present with that person relationally.

To be present involves a movement away from oneself. It involves being "ecstatic," to pick up a term Zizioulas uses to describe the overcoming of one's boundaries which is necessary for communion.[48] Boff describes presence as "sending a message to another in the expectation and hope of being heard and accepted while at the same time hearing and receiving a message from the other."[49] Volf uses the term "self-donation" to refer to this giving of oneself that marks presence. In describing trinitarian self-donation, he states, "the self gives something of itself, of its own space, so to speak, in a movement in which it contracts itself in order to be expanded by the other and in which it at the same time enters the contracted other in order to increase the other's plenitude."[50] Being present to the other by moving toward the other is part of what it means to exist perichoretically.

Humans cannot simply repeat the self-giving that marks the presence of the Trinity. As Volf points out, the intra-trinitarian self-donation is mutual and simultaneous.[51] In human relationships on this side of the eschaton, reciprocal and simultaneous self-donation seldom exists, if ever. We cannot perfectly mirror the self-donation that characterizes the trinitarian relations. What we *are* called to mirror is the self-donation that the Trinity directs toward humanity. This is a one-sided type of love "that seeks to elicit the non-existent response of love in those who practice the very opposite of love."[52] The perfect love within the Trinity becomes suffering love when it is directed toward humanity. It is this self-donation in the form of suffering love that we are called to imitate. The imperative to do to others as we would have them do to us (Matt 7:12; Luke 6:31) points to an ideal of reciprocity for which we yearn, but reciprocity is not

---

48. Zizioulas uses this term in relation to both divine and human persons. Zizioulas, *Being as Communion*, 44–46. Grenz provides a helpful discussion of Zizioulas on this point. See Grenz, *Rediscovering the Triune God*, 139.

49. Boff, *Trinity and Society*, 129.

50. Volf, "'The Trinity Is Our Social Program,'" 412.

51. Ibid., 413.

52. Ibid.

a condition of such love. The community of believers should be known by its willingness to love unilaterally.

The presence found in the Trinity is also characterized by openness. Being open to the other is a necessity for communing.[53] The Trinity is not only open internally, but is open also to the world. Moltmann argues, "through the sending of the creative Spirit, the trinitarian history of God becomes a history that is open to the world, open to men and women, and open to the future."[54] The church is to reflect this openness.

The trinitarian openness that characterizes presence is ecclesiologically formative in at least three ways. First, each local church must be open to the unfolding history of the world. It is an openness that takes in and bears the suffering of the world in a manner that imitates the way in which the Trinity takes in the world's suffering. The church must not seal itself off from the world. Second, this openness means that not just world history in general but concrete individuals outside the church are welcomed in. The church is to be open to all without prior judgment, though as Volf wants to make clear, this does not mean embracing evil as well as good.[55] The *will* to give ourselves to others, which is how we embrace others, is that to which the people of God are called. For the church as a corporate body to be open, individuals who comprise that body must be open. This means that the friendships of those within the church may not be limited just to other Christians or to those with whom we share an affinity, for Moltmann is right when he says, "Christian friendship cannot be lived in the inner circle of one's equals but only in open affection and public respect for other people."[56] A third way the openness of the Trinity relates to ecclesiology has to do with the way local churches relate to each other. As Volf argues, churches must be open to one another.[57] This open-

53. It is interesting to note that Boff prefers to refer to "communing" rather than "communion" because the former is active, and what he is talking about only exists in the practice of a relationship. See Boff, *Trinity and Society*, 129.

54. Moltmann, *The Trinity and the Kingdom*, 90.

55. He argues that "an indiscriminate welcome of everyone by no means entails an indiscriminate affirmation of everything" (Volf, "'The Trinity Is Our Social Program,'" 416).

56. Moltmann, *The Trinity and the Kingdom*, 120.

57. Volf refers to this openness as the ecclesial minimum for the catholicity of the church. He goes on to note that if an openness to other churches is *all* that can be said about a church, its catholicity would be poor. The minimum is not the optimum. Volf, *After Our Likeness*, 275.

ness is a foretaste of the complete communion unity that will mark the body of Christ in the end.

This presence, which is characterized by self-donation and openness, calls into question any structures that create boundaries in the church. When clerical identity shuts a person off from others in the body of Christ, it must be redefined. Forms of congregational leadership that caution against "getting too close" to parishioners must be questioned in light of the trinitarian presence we are to mirror. Pastors should be the leading examples of relational presence and openness.

All Christians are called to be present with others—both others in the church and others outside the church. A presence marked by self-donation and openness should characterize those who lead the church as well as those who assume other roles in the church. We do not find certain Christians called to be present while other Christians are exempt from it. *All* Christians are to mirror the trinitarian presence. The fact that all the people of God are to be present with others through self-donation and openness calls for an understanding of the royal priesthood as self-giving.

Equality

The relations within the Trinity are characterized by equalness. Each Person in the Trinity participates equally in the other two. No single Person in the Trinity is more fully in relation than the other two. Moltmann says this about the perichoretic unity of the Trinity: "here the three Persons are equal; they live and are manifested in one another and through one another."[58] The perichoretic nature of the Trinity supports this claim for equalness in the trinitarian relations. The Father, Son, and Holy Spirit are always mutually and equally related. Volf makes the point in this way: "in a community of perfect love between persons who share all divine attributes a notion of hierarchy is unintelligible."[59] Within the Trinity no one Person has more power than the others, no one Person is more privileged than the others, and no one Person is more worthy of greater honor and praise. The three Persons of the Trinity share completely in all these things.

58. Moltmann, *The Trinity and the Kingdom*, 176.

59. Volf, "'The Trinity Is Our Social Program,'" 407.

Are we justified in extrapolating from the nature of the Trinity to the nature of the church on this point? Could a limit to correspondence exist here? Could not the nature of our creatureliness require a form of relationships within the church that is disjunctive with the inter-trinitarian equality?

One might argue that, given the fallen nature of humans, social structures cannot work with equalness in relations, so even if the Trinity is not monarchial, a monarchial pattern might be necessary in the church. Such an argument must be rejected though, because the witness of Scripture points to correspondence at this point, not disjunction. Jesus admonished his disciples to let no one call them rabbi or teacher (Matt 23:8–11), because of the way this would contribute to relational unequalness (v. 11). Carrying forward this relational understanding marked by equality, Paul rebukes those who would maintain economic and social divisions at the Lord's supper (1 Cor 11:17–22).[60] The teaching of Jesus, applied by Paul, is that stratified relations are not acceptable within the body of Christ. The argument for disjunction at this point between the Trinity and the church is not sustainable. The inter-trinitarian equality is *not* disjunctive with our creaturely existence. The church *is* supposed to reflect the equality present in the trinitarian relations. Pyramidal or hierarchical models of the church must therefore be put aside. The nature of the Trinity calls for an egalitarian church structure, a church structure marked by equalness.

If the church is to be marked by equality, no cultic stratification is acceptable. Such stratification must be set aside as our understanding of the priesthood of all believers is pressed into the egalitarian image of the Trinity.

Non-domination

The trinitarian relations are characterized by non-domination. The relations are consensual and free. No one Person in the Trinity dictates what the other Persons must do. No one Person of the Trinity forces the others to participate in the relationships or to act in certain ways. No one Person of the Trinity imposes decisions upon the other Persons.

Non-domination must characterize the life of the church as well. Moltmann makes the case that dominating rulership by the church and

---

60. Cf. Yoder's discussion of the Lord's supper in *Body Politics*, 14–27.

the state has been justified based on a hierarchical view of the Trinity.[61] A perichoretic understanding of the Trinity rules out such domination. A perichoretic understanding of the Trinity "constitutes the church as 'a community free of dominion.'"[62] To the extent that the church is characterized by non-domination, it provides a foretaste of the eschatological social arrangements.

The narratives of Jesus point to this characteristic of non-domination in the Trinity. This is seen powerfully in Jesus' act of washing his disciples' feet (John 13:1–21) where his servant posture is the antithesis of domination. We also see this where he points to the domination present in the existing social structures of his day and then tells his disciples that in the social structure he is ushering in the greatest shall be servants (Luke 22:24–27). Domination is not the way of the kingdom.

All Jesus's relationships were marked by freedom. Jesus did not coerce anyone to follow him and he did not force anyone to remain in his company. He had a clear picture of a preferred future for all of humanity, but he didn't foist this upon anyone. His disciples were to follow his pattern of non-domination. Walter Wink notes that this theme of non-domination was pervasive in Jesus's message. Wink makes this summary observation: "Jesus is not looking for a kingdom for himself or anyone else where power can be wielded in order to *impose* God's will on the world. He is inaugurating a domination-free society."[63] The church should be modeled on the Trinity in this way and should be a model for a domination-free society.

The freedom that marks the trinitarian pattern of non-domination relates to church membership as well. The Anabaptist tradition made a major contribution to ecclesiology by insisting that church membership be voluntary. No one should be coerced into becoming a church member and no one should be forced to remain a member. The Free Church tradition derives its name in part from this very point. Participation in the church must be freely chosen, just as the trinitarian communion is marked by freedom.

The non-domination that marks the Trinity has direct implications for ecclesial leadership. Authoritarian and dictatorial approaches to lead-

---

61. Moltmann, *The Trinity and the Kingdom*, 192–200.

62. Ibid., 202.

63. Wink, "The Kingdom," 163 (emphasis original).

ership have no place within our ecclesial structures. Our churches cannot adopt military and certain corporate models of leadership. Only forms of leadership that are non-dominating are appropriate for church leaders.

Unity

Unity marks the Trinity. While relational approaches to the Trinity do not begin by focusing on this unity, nonetheless any given view of the Trinity must show how the trinitarian unity coexists with relationships if this view is to be viable. Perichoresis is one means of establishing the trinitarian unity. Moltmann, for example, sees the unity of the Trinity as tied to the mutual indwelling and reciprocal interpenetration of the Father, Son, and Holy Spirit.[64] Similarly, Volf asserts, "it is advisable to dispense entirely with the one numerically identical divine nature and instead to conceive of the unity of God *perichoretically.*"[65]

The unity that marks the Trinity is a unity that is to mark the church, and perichoresis is helpful in understanding the church's unity as well. Mutual indwelling is the ground of our unity as Christians. A human cannot be interior to another human as subject in the same way that the Persons of the Trinity are interior to one another;[66] we can enter into the experience of another empathically but we cannot fully indwell one another, so perichoretic human relations cannot serve as the basis for ecclesial unity. The unity of the church is achieved not through perichoretic human relations but through our perichoretic relations with God. In John 17:22–23 we overhear Jesus praying to the Father and these are his words: "The glory that you have given me I have given them, so that they may be one, as we are one, I in them and you in me, that they may become com-

64. Moltmann, *The Trinity and the Kingdom*, viii.

65. Volf, *After Our Likeness*, 203. Perichoresis need not stand alone as the only basis for the unity of God. Moltmann adds two other bases: the "monarchial" unity brought about by the Father, and a "uniting mutuality and community [that] proceeds from *the Holy Spirit*" (Moltmann, *The Trinity and the Kingdom*, 177–78). Pannenberg gives a nod to the unifying nature of perichoresis (319, 334), though he, as does Moltmann, points to the monarchy of the Father and describes it as "the seal of their unity" (Pannenberg, *Systematic Theology*, 325). Pannenberg does not stop here, but continues on to ground the unity of the Trinity in the divine actions characterized by love (Grenz, *Rediscovering the Triune God*, 100). I am not arguing that perichoresis is the *only* basis for unity, but rather, that it is at least *one of* the bases for trinitarian unity.

66. Volf, *After Our Likeness*, 210–12.

pletely one . . . ." We are also told that God's Spirit dwells in us, and that we are in the Spirit (Rom 8:9; cf. 1 Cor 3:16; 2 Tim 1:14). This indwelling is reflective of the perichoresis within the Trinity and is the ground for our unity as Christians. We relate perichoretically to each other through the Son as represented by the Spirit. While our relations with the Spirit do not correspond exactly to the inter-trinitarian relations because "the interiority of the divine persons is strictly reciprocal, which is not the case in the relation between God and human beings,"[67] this qualification does not negate our perichoretic relations with the Spirit.

If a person is in the Spirit, and the Spirit is in another person, then a form of person-to-person indwelling *does* exist, what I suggest we call a *"mediated* indwelling." It does not have the fullness of the indwelling found within the Trinity, but it is an indwelling nonetheless. Volf describes this person-to-person indwelling as the "interiority of personal characteristics" which leads to unity in this way:

> In personal encounters, that which the other person is flows consciously and unconsciously into that which I am. The reverse is also true. In this mutual giving and receiving, we give to others not only something, but also a piece of ourselves, something of that which we have made of ourselves in communion with others; and from others we take not only something, but also a piece of them. Each person gives of himself or herself to others, and each person in a unique way takes up others into himself or herself. This is the process of mutual internalization of personal characteristics occurring in the church through the Holy Spirit indwelling Christians.[68]

The Spirit allows for the mutual internalization of personal characteristics, which helps ground the unity of the church.

If unity is part of ecclesiality, then a form of it must be found that allows for the current existence of the church in this day and age when complete inter-communion unity is lacking. Volf suggests that the pre-eschatological unity of the church is found in the openness of every local church to all other churches. This does not adequately describe the final and full condition of the people of God, but "this openness to all other

67. Ibid., 211.

68. Ibid., 211–12.

churches is the *interecclesial minimum* of the concrete proleptic experience of the eschatological gathering of the whole people of God."[69]

If the Trinity is the ground for ecclesial unity in this way, then Moltmann may be right in rejecting the monarchial episcopate as the ground for ecclesial unity.[70] He argues that papal authority can indeed bring about unity in the church, but it is not an adequate type of unity. The monarchial episcopate can maintain the unity of the church as institution, but this in no way assures the unity of the church as community. Communal unity, the unity of the royal priesthood, requires not a monarchial episcopate, but mutual indwelling mediated by the Holy Spirit.

To summarize, the unity of the church is achieved through perichoresis. As the church participates in the Spirit—as Christians are indwelt by the Spirit, indwell the Spirit, and through the Spirit indwell one another—the unity of the church is established. It is in this way that Christians become one as Jesus Christ and the Father are one (John 17:11).

Differentiation

Unity presupposes differentiation; if no differences exist, we have nothing to unite. Relationships also presuppose differentiation. The relationships within the Trinity require a differentiation of persons. As Moltmann puts it, "each of the Persons possesses the divine nature in a non-interchangeable way; each presents it in his own way."[71] This means that they share in the divine nature, and yet the Persons have their own uniqueness also. This differentiation is reflected in the differentiation of actions. For example, the Father creates, the Son gives himself up, and the Spirit breathes and glorifies. Volf, too, argues that in order for perichoretic indwelling to occur, difference must exist, for one cannot indwell oneself.[72] The unity of the Trinity coexists with and requires diversity.

The church is to reflect the diversity found in the Trinity. This celebration of diversity is powerfully attested to in the diversity of languages that flowed forth from the Christian community in Jerusalem on the day of Pentecost (Acts 2:4). The diversity which marked the people of God at

69. Ibid., 157–58.

70. Moltmann, *The Trinity and the Kingdom*, 200–202.

71. Moltmann, *The Trinity and the Kingdom*, 171.

72. Volf, *After Our Likeness*, 209.

Pentecost stands in stark contrast to the homogenizing forces at work in Babel (Gen 11) and prefigures the diversity to be found in the eschatological kingdom of God (Rev 7:9; 14:6). The people of God are united in Christ through the Spirit, and at the same time these people are marked by great diversity.

By looking at the nature of the Trinity, we are able to more clearly understand the nature of the church. We must see relationality, presence, equality, non-domination, unity, and differentiation in the nature of the church if the church is to correspond to the Trinity.

CHARISMS

The charisms bestowed by the Spirit on the people of God are a point of concrete trinitarian correspondence in the church. The nature of the Trinity is imprinted on the charisms. I shall now set forth my understanding of the charisms.[73] I suggest that an ecclesiology connected to this understanding of the charisms leads to an egalitarian and participatory model of the priesthood of all believers.

Pneumatological

The charisms are connected to the Trinity from the start because they are given by the third Person of the Trinity, the Holy Spirit (1 Cor 12:4–11). The Spirit freely distributes charisms when and where the Spirit so chooses. The distribution of charisms has an interactional aspect to it as seen by the fact that we are instructed to strive for them (1 Cor 12:31; 14:1),[74] but weight must still fall on the fact that the Spirit is the one who distributes these gifts. No person or church can decide which gifts will be bestowed upon whom. Nor can any person or church decide *when* the Spirit will bestow a gift. Therefore, Volf is on track when he says, "this clearly reveals

73. Vatican II affirms several of the characteristics of charisms that are set forth here. In *Lumen Gentium* we see affirmations that the Holy Spirit is the giver of these gifts, that these gifts are spread among *all* the faithful, and that these gifts are to be used for the building up of the body of Christ, in accordance with 1 Cor 12:7. Part of the responsibility of office holders is to identify the gifts of the faithful and to empower them to use these gifts. A result of this emphasis on the universal distribution and purpose of charisms is that the laity are given a significant role in the mission of Christ. The charisms of office, though, remain distinct. See "*Lumen Gentium,*" §12.

74. Cf. Volf, *After Our Likeness*, 233.

that the church lives from a dynamic not deriving from itself . . . . It is not the church that 'organizes' its life, but rather the Holy Spirit."[75]

The pneumatological nature of the charisms highlights the pneumatological nature of the church. Structure is essential to the life of the church and can provide effective conduits through which the Spirit might work. But while essential, church structure is in constant need of renewal because it always moves towards calcification and rigidity, which tries to contain the movement of the Spirit. Conceptions of the priesthood of all believers eventually fall into this rigid and calcified state.[76] We need to promote ecclesial structures that have enough freedom and opportunity in and around them to allow for the Spirit to work in an unrestricted manner. Steffen Lösel points to the liturgy as a place where we can look for the Spirit to be present and to guide the community. He suggests that it is in the assembly of Christian worship, in the gaps between the holy things and the people, that the Spirit moves and works.[77] His approach shows how the Spirit can be at work through more defined ecclesial structures; churches do not have to be marked by informal or minimal structure to allow for the Spirit to work. Structures are not irrelevant, but the more important issue is whether or not a given structure is used with a sensitivity to and expectation of the Holy Spirit. For example, a highly structured Catholic church can be more open to the Spirit than an informally structured Free Church. The acceptability of a given church structure is connected to its ability to reflect the pneumatological nature of the church.

The pneumatological nature of the charisms is also evidenced in their "diachronic plurality," a phrase Volf uses to mean that various charismata can replace one another over time.[78] A person might be given the charism of hospitality, and then, a few years down the road, as the Spirit sees fit, this charism might be replaced with the charism of teaching.[79] Volf claims,

---

75. Ibid., 232.

76. Therefore, even if the church fully embraces the conception I am setting forth, at some point it, too, will need to be refreshed and revised.

77. Lösel, "Guidance from the Gaps."

78. Volf, *After Our Likeness*, 233.

79. Romans 11:29 at first glance might be seen to contradict this with the statement that "the gifts and the calling of God are irrevocable." But the gifts referred to in this passage are not the charisms of the Spirit, but the covenant which God made with the Israelites, an expression of his calling. While that type of gift in the form of covenant

"over the history of the congregation and of its individual members, the charismata with which these members serve in the congregation can . . . change."[80] The diachronic nature of the charisms is consistent with the fluid nature of the Spirit's work. The Spirit who freely grants charisms is just as free to take them away and replace them with others. Given the pneumatological nature of the charisms, our ecclesiology cannot assume their permanence.

Universal

Charisms are universally distributed by the Spirit to all believers (1 Cor 12:7; cf. Rom 12:3; Eph 4:7; 1 Pet 4:10). Not every believer chooses to *exercise* his or her gift(s), but there is no such thing as a Christian who has not been gifted by the Spirit. Because all members of the church are so gifted, all members of the church share a common responsibility for the church, just as each member of the Trinity shares responsibility for the life of the Trinity. The Spirit may indeed grant more than one gift at a time to a person, something Volf refers to as the "synchronic plurality" of the charisms.[81] However, while a person might have more than one gift, *no* person has *all* the gifts. The charisms come to full expression only when all the people are using their gifts.

This interdependence does not rule out office, but it *does* rule out a do-it-all type of leadership. Such a form of leadership, according to Volf, "would lead to the hypertrophy of this one member of the body of Christ and to a fateful atrophy of all other members."[82] The universal distribution of gifts means that no Christian should be passive because *all* the people of God have things to contribute to the body.[83] No member of the Trinity takes on more responsibility than the other members, and no member of the Trinity is passive while the others are active. Correspondingly, all

---

calling is irrevocable, this irrevocability is nowhere applied to the charisms.

80. Volf, *After Our Likeness*, 233.

81. Ibid.

82. Ibid., 230.

83. Vatican II saw this connection also: "From the reception of these charisms, even the most ordinary ones, there arises for each of the faithful the right and duty of exercising them in the Church and in the world for the good of men and the development of the Church..." ("*Apostolicam Actuositatem*," §3). Of course this same statement points to a hierarchy of charisms (some are "ordinary" while others are not) which is at odds with the equal value of all charisms for which I contend.

believers share in the responsibility for the life of the church. The universal distribution of charisms necessitates a participatory ecclesiology, one in which all members—each in accordance with his or her particular gifts—work together for the building up of the body of Christ.

Diverse

The Spirit gifts people in diverse ways. This diversity is suggested by the variety of gifts included in the several lists found in Scripture (Rom 12:6–8; 1 Cor 12:28–30; Eph 4:11; 1 Pet 4:10–11). In writing about these lists, Fee argues that they were not intended to be exhaustive,[84] so the diversity of gifts might go even beyond what is listed. Here the trinitarian differentiation finds correspondence. As it is of the Trinity, differentiation is an internal characteristic of the charisms. The people of the church are called to differentiated activities. Because of their differing charisms, the members of the church are not identical in their functions; rather, they are diverse.

United

Unity exists simultaneously with this diversity, again corresponding to the Trinity. The diverse gifts are united because they are all part of one body, the body of Christ (1 Cor 12). The charisms are united in their common purpose which is to build up the body (Eph 4:12b).[85] The building up of the body requires the charisms to function interdependently. Because no one person has all the charisms, the full expression of charisms requires the mutual activity of the entire community. Paul points to this when he states, in a section on charisms, that "individually we are members one of another" (Rom 12:5). This interdependence is also seen in Paul's use of the body analogy (1 Cor 12). He points to the diversity by saying, "the body does not consist of one member but of many" (v. 14), and he ties this diversity into a unity: "there are many members, yet one body" (v. 20). The unity in diversity is highlighted in v. 27 where Paul writes, "now

---

84. Gordon Fee, *God's Empowering Presence: The Holy Spirit in the Letters of Paul*, 886.

85. In *"Apostolicam Actuositatem,"* Vatican II affirmed the unified purpose of the diverse gifts: "In the Church there is diversity of ministry but unity of mission" (§2).

you are the body of Christ [unity] and individually [diversity] members of it [unity]."

Mutual

Volf asserts that because the charisms are interdependent, the life of the church must be characterized by mutuality.[86] Such mutual giving and receiving corresponds to the type of relationality found in the Trinity. Mutuality marks *all* the charisms, including those normally associated with office. The Spirit of Christ is present in each charism, and so each person who uses a charism is acting as a representative of the Christ who is in the charism. This representation is a mutual activity. Therefore, Volf contends, "spiritual activity and receptivity are no longer assigned to two different groups of persons, but rather represent two basic activities of every person; that is, every person acts *in persona Christi* and every person receives this activity."[87] This does not eliminate the need for office holders, but it does mean that "their actions do not differ in principle from those of any other member of the church."[88] The mutuality of the trinitarian relations "finds its correspondence in the image of the church in which *all* members serve one another with their specific gifts of the Spirit."[89] The charisms point to the mutuality of the whole of ecclesial life.

Egalitarian

The charisms are marked by an equality of value. No charism can be claimed to be of greater importance that the others. This is the whole thrust of Paul's argument regarding the importance of each part of the body (1 Cor 12). It is true that in 1 Cor 12:31 the readers are exhorted to "strive for the greater gifts," a statement that has sometimes been taken to mean that some gifts are of more value than others.[90] However, Gordon Fee asserts, "the difficulties with this view . . . are too numerous to make it viable."[91] For one, as just previously noted, such an interpretation goes

---

86. Volf, *After Our Likeness*, 231.

87. Ibid.

88. Ibid., 231.

89. Ibid., 219.

90. E.g., Küng, *The Church*, 504–5.

91. Fee, *God's Empowering Presence*, 195.

against the whole flow of Paul's argument.[92] Like Fee, Yoder concludes that a hierarchy of gifts must be ruled out. He argues that in 1 Cor 12, Paul is asserting that the gifts can*not* be prioritized. Yoder states, "this warning is not marginal; it is the point of the passage . . . . Paul's whole concern is that it be recognized that *all* these many gifts have the same source, and that all are (each in its place) of the same value."[93] Because charisms are *not* prioritized, and because Paul is arguing for the importance of *all* parts of the body, I assert that no charism is more important than any other; all charisms are of equal value. We have seen how the Trinity is marked by equality, and now we see this mirrored in the church. Just as no Person of the Trinity can be said to be more important than the others, so no charism—and no possessor of a charism—can be said to be of more importance than the others. Every charism is of equal value in its own way. This must emerge in an egalitarian priesthood of all believers. No priest within this royal priesthood is more important than any of the other priests.

Outward-oriented

The trinitarian presence is marked by movement toward the other, and this same movement is found in the charisms. The charisms are never self-directed; that is, they are never focused on personal benefit. The charisms are always directed toward the good of the community. Believers become present with each other as they use their charisms to move outward for the sake of others. In this way the charisms bring believers into trinitarian correspondence.

The charisms vivify the church. The nature of the Trinity and the witness of Scripture combine to show that the charisms are pneumatological, universal, diverse, united, relational, egalitarian, and outward-oriented. As believers use their charisms, these characteristics should shape the life and structures of the church. These characteristics give specific shape to the royal priesthood.

---

92. Fee sets forth several other reasons that the prioritization of gifts cannot be what Paul meant to communicate, and then he goes on to suggest three possibilities for what Paul *did* in fact mean here. See Ibid.

93. Yoder, *Fullness*, 10.

ORDINATION

"[A]n entire ecclesiology is always reflected in a certain understanding of office, that is, of what officeholders are to do in the church and how they are to become officeholders," writes Volf.[94] The veracity of his statement requires more in-depth exploration of the issue of ordination. Ordination is normally associated with installation into a ministerial priesthood. But if such a priesthood is not justified, what is the nature of ordination? Ordination is a rite of recognition and blessing which should be administered to *all* the people of God. To substantiate this assertion we will consider the nature of ordination from several different angles. First, I will look at the relationship of the laying on of hands to ordination. I suggest that the traditional relationship posited between the laying on of hands and ordination is not the most natural relationship that emerges from the texts. This opens up the possibility of re-conceiving ordination. The nature of the charisms provides a second angle from which to approach ordination. The charism of office has traditionally been seen as directly tied to ordination—ordination is either confirmation of this charism or the rite by which this charism is granted. However, based on my understanding of the nature of the charisms, I suggest that the charism of office (or the charisms associated with office) cannot be distinguished from other charisms, and therefore ordination should be oriented toward *all* the charisms, not just a select few. Third, we find fundamental agreement that the church is to be marked by unity. But what is the basis of this unity? The Catholic tradition sees the ordained priesthood as key. I suggest that our perichoretic relationships with and through the Spirit are our ground for unity. This requires that ordination be conceived of as something other than installation into a unifying function. That function does not rightly belong to a select few in the church. Finally, I suggest that Christian community, not office, is central to ecclesiality. A ramification of this is that ordination does not place priests at the center of the church because the community is already there, and therefore the question of what ordination *does* accomplish is open for reconsideration. With these four points as justification, I offer an alternative view of ordination. By interacting with Catholic, mainline, and Free Church voices, I attempt to set forth a theology that is ecumenically sensitive, even if not ecumenically embraced.

94. Volf, *After Our Likeness*, 221.

Laying on of Hands in the NT

The NT passages that describe the laying on of hands have been used as the basis for a theology of ordination.[95] In order to begin to reconsider this idea, we will consider each relevant passage and their implications for installation to office.

In Acts 6:1–6 we are told of Hellenists complaining of distributive injustice at the hands of the Hebrews. In response, the community chose seven men to oversee the proper distribution of food, and following their selection the apostles laid hands on them. We are told that these men were appointed for a specific task (v. 3). This was not a lifetime appointment to an office. The apostles instructed the *community* to select these men (vv. 2–3). The idea of appointing some to a task of distributing food "pleased the whole community" (v. 5). These appointments were not imposed upon the community, but emerged from within and with the approval of the community.

Two chapters later, Peter and John come and lay their hands on the crowds to whom Philip has been preaching, and the people receive the Holy Spirit (Acts 8:5, 14–17). This laying on of hands was not an installation to office—the crowds were not made into bishops or priests. Here the laying on of hands is the means by which the Spirit is given, but in other places the Spirit comes upon people *without* the laying on of hands (e.g., Acts 2:4; 4:31; 10:44; Mark 1:10) so this passage cannot be said to describe a normative means of receiving the Spirit. Though this passage is not addressing the granting of charisms, I suggest that the Spirit works in the same way in distributing charisms: the Spirit *may* choose to bestow a charism through the laying on of hands, but the laying on of hands does not *guarantee* this action by the Spirit. The Spirit remains free to bestow charisms upon believers in any number of other ways as well.

Still later in Acts we are told about Barnabas and Saul returning from a particular mission (Acts 12:25—13:4). They are then assigned another mission and are sent out through the laying on of hands. The word translated here as "set apart" can also be translated as "appoint," a translation that gives a clearer sense of the meaning here. This idea of setting apart has mistakenly been taken to mean a setting apart from the rest of the community. But Barnabas and Saul were not set apart from the commu-

95. For a detailed treatment of the relevant passages and the theological understandings of ordination that have arisen from them, see Warkentin, *Ordination*, 109–56.

nity and placed into a special category of Christians. They were set apart in the sense that they were appointed to a specific task. Just as hands were laid upon them for this specific task, so hands may have been laid upon them as they embarked on their previous mission and hands may have been laid on them as they set out on future missions. The appointment in this passage is to a specific task, not a lifelong office.

When Paul came to Ephesus, he asked if the disciples there had received the Holy Spirit (Acts 19:1–2). He indicates that the reception of the Holy Spirit upon conversion is normative (v. 2). That the Ephesians had *not* received the Spirit at conversion seems anomalous. This situation was rectified when Paul laid hands on them and the Holy Spirit came upon them (v. 6). The laying on of hands is connected to the coming of the Spirit, but the laying on of hands here is not part of an appointment to a particular task, much less to the particular task of officeholder.

In the letters to Timothy, we find two references to the laying on of hands (1 Tim 4:12–15; 2 Tim 1:5–7). These two passages—which may refer to the same event or two different events—speak of a gift that Timothy has received through the laying on of hands. While it is not completely clear what this gift is, it may be the gift of public reading, exhorting, and teaching, or it may be the gift of faith.[96] Whatever the gift is, it does not constitute grounds for a permanent structure of office. Marjorie Warkentin, in her excellent examination of the biblical-historical grounding for ordination, examines these passages and concludes, "the laying on of hands on Timothy is not a rite initiated by the apostolic church with a view for setting a normative pattern for induction into pastoral or missionary roles."[97]

A final reference to the laying on of hands is found in Heb 6:1–2. Since the whole book of Hebrews builds on the OT, the author may have been referring here to the OT practice of laying hands on people in connection to commissioning people for public service or to the sacrificial rituals.[98] If this is the case, then the practice may have a negative connotation in this context—the author (who is calling for the readers to grow up) may be alluding to a contrast between OT priests who were designated by the laying on of hands and Jesus who is appointed high

96 Fee, *1 and 2 Timothy, Titus*, 108.

97. Warkentin, *Ordination*, 142. The same conclusion is reached by Schatzmann, *A Pauline Theology of Charismata*, 49–50.

98. Bruce, *The Epistle to the Hebrews*, 142–43.

priest by God.[99] Another possibility is that the author was drawing on the established association in the early church between the laying on of hands and the impartation of the Holy Spirit.[100] We cannot establish that the laying on of hands here refers to installation in a special priesthood in the church.

The laying on of hands in the NT is sometimes connected to a specific ministry task and sometimes connected to the coming of the Holy Spirit. While the Holy Spirit on some occasions came upon people through the laying on of hands, not every instance of the laying on of hands is tied to the coming of the Spirit. Also, the Spirit came upon people *without* the laying on of hands. No where is the laying on of hands tied to installation into a hierarchical office. While these passages have been used to argue for a theology of ordination that is reflective of a hierarchical ecclesial structure, such a usage reads back into the texts an understanding of office that simply did not exist at the time. This look at the NT texts does not settle the issue, for even if textual evidence does not exist for the traditional view of ordination in the church, the matter remains open for theological development. In the sections that follow, I point to the theological reasons we should affirm the NT trajectory seen in this section.

Charisms and Ordination to Office

We must recognize a distinction between charisms—including those commonly associated with the pastoral role, such as the charisms of leadership, preaching, teaching, and pastoring—and office. I hold that charisms and office are related, but not identical, so I do not refer to "the charism of office" as is common in many traditions. Most individuals who are ordained to pastoral office will likely have charisms such as the gift of leadership and the gift of preaching. People ordained to pastoral office will in general, then, have charisms that differ from *many* of those who are not ordained to such a ministry or office, but not necessarily different from *all* who are not ordained for this role. And, while certain charisms will naturally be concentrated among those who are ordained to congregational ministry, even within this group a diversity of gifts exists. One person in this group might have a primary gifting in the area of preaching

99. Lane, *Hebrews 1–8*, 140.
100. Hagner, *Hebrews*, 87–88.

while another might have a primary gifting in the area of administration and yet another in counseling. Office should not be equated exactly with any particular charism.

Because of the essential commonality of all the charisms, believers participate in one and only one priesthood, the royal priesthood. A second priesthood reserved for those with only certain charisms must be ruled out. Vatican II affirms a royal priesthood, but argues for a second priesthood as well, a priesthood of the ordained.[101] This ministerial or hierarchical priesthood "differs essentially and not only in degree"[102] from the common priesthood. Office is transmitted through episcopal consecration.[103] BEM keeps the ordained ministry more closely tied to the community. Rather than an essential difference, BEM asserts what might be called an "essential commonality"—the ordained and the lay are "interrelated."[104] Authorization comes not from apostolic succession, but from the recognition, support, and encouragement of the community, apart from which the ministerial priesthood has no existence.[105] The ordained retain a special role, though, for the ministry of the ordained "is constitutive for the life and witness of the Church."[106] I agree with Vatican II and BEM that a priesthood exists which includes all believers (1 Peter 2:5, 9). It is on the validity of a second priesthood, a special priesthood for the ordained, that I must take my leave from this fine company.[107] The church is *not* composed of two priesthoods; it is *not* composed of the priesthood of all believers and a ministerial priesthood. The essential commonality of all the charisms points to a *single* priesthood in which *all* believers function as priests through the use of their diverse and egalitarian charisms.

While I embrace much of Volf's ecclesiological project, I believe he takes an unfortunate turn when, in discussing ordination, he asserts that

101. For example, see *"Presbyterorum Ordinis"* where it states that priests are "made sharers in a *special way* in Christ's priesthood" (my italics), and they alone exercise Christ's "priestly function for our benefit" (§5).

102. *"Lumen Gentium,"* §10.

103. Ibid., §21.

104. "Ministry/BEM," §12.

105. Ibid., §12.

106. Ibid., §8.

107. Of course, all of us agree on a third priesthood: the unique priesthood of Christ which is distinct from any priesthood composed of humans.

the charisms of office are different from other charisms,[108] a position in concurrence with the voices of Vatican II and BEM. Volf states that the charisms of office are different from other charisms because they involve service to or on behalf of the entire local congregation.[109] I suggest that this is not quite accurate. I suggest that there is no proper use of *any* charism that does *not* serve or represent the *whole* community.

The proper use of *any* spiritual gift is a service to the entire body. A person using her spiritual gifts in relation to another person is in fact always serving the whole community because, as each act is carried out, whether in the context of a one-on-one relationship or in the context of the broader community, the act is carried out upon Christ. And because the church is the body of Christ, the act is therefore carried out upon the church as well. All uses of charisms serve the community as a whole. Trying to draw a line between those that are of greater service and those that are of lesser service is not possible.

The proper use of any spiritual gift is also always carried out on behalf of the entire body. Concerning catholicity, Volf argues that every believer is a catholic person "because the whole Christ indwells every one through the Holy Spirit."[110] A logical extension of this, which Volf does not make, is to say that when a person uses her spiritual gifts, she represents the whole Christ within her. And if she represents the whole Christ who indwells her, then she represents all others who are bound up in that whole Christ. When a man acts compassionately towards his brother who is suffering, he is representing or acting on behalf of the entire body of Christ. Therefore the charisms cannot be divided into the categories of corporate and personal. They are *all* corporate *and* personal.

Another problem arises out of Volf's statement that charisms of office are referenced to the "entirety of the local church."[111] What is the "entirety" of the local church? If a local congregation usually has seventy-five people who gather to worship on most Sundays, but on a particular Sunday only twenty gather, does this gathering constitute the entirety of the local church at that time and in that place, or does this gathering con-

---

108. Volf, *After Our Likeness*, 246–47. At the same time, he maintains that there is "no difference in principle between officeholders and other members of the church" (Volf, *After Our Likeness*, 246).

109. Volf, *After Our Likeness*, 247.

110. Ibid., 279.

111. Ibid., 247.

stitute only part of a church? According to the main thrust of Volf's argu-
mentation in *After Our Likeness*, this gathering of twenty would constitute
a whole church, not just a partial or "less than entire" church. I fully agree
with Volf's view that where two or three are gathered in Christ's name,
there is the church (Matt 18:20). Flowing from this conviction, I suggest
that any charism used by one believer in relation to even just one other
believer is a charism referenced to the entirety of the local church in that
time and location. In this particular place where Volf speaks about office
and ordination, he uses this phrase "the entirety of the local church" in
a way that seems to imply that where just a few are gathered, the entire
local church may *not* be present. I suggest that this is inconsistent with his
more foundational position regarding the nature of the church.

If we decide that charisms cannot be divided up between those that
are referenced to the entire congregation and those that are not, and if we
hold to Volf's conviction that the church is present wherever two or three
are gathered in Christ's name, then ordination can no longer be associated with only certain charisms based on their reference to the entirety of
the local church.

Source of Unity

Is church office, along with the Holy Spirit, a valid basis for ecclesial
unity? *Lumen Gentium* identifies both these as sources of church unity.[112]
The ordained are the concrete expression of unity and it is in them that
the other believers are united. BEM also points to the ordained as a focus
of the church's unity.[113] But I suggest that, because our unity is grounded
perichoretically in the Trinity through the Holy Spirit, the ordained
priesthood is *not* essential for our unity. A result of this position is that
the clergy no longer have a special status because of an intrinsic unifying
function. Because unity is grounded fundamentally in the Holy Spirit and
not in office, the latter is not part of the essence of the church.[114] Certainly
most ordained persons contribute to the concrete expression of the unity

---

112. "*Lumen Gentium*," §11.

113. "Ministry/BEM," §21.

114. Volf rightly points out that some form of office, even if only implicit, is necessary for the enduring vitality of the church. (Volf, *After Our Likeness*, 248). This does not
mean, however, that office and the charisms associated with it are essential in a way that
other charisms are not.

we have in the Spirit. But this is a result of the Holy Spirit indwelling them, not a result of their office. Since the Holy Spirit, and not office, is the source of unity for the church, the nature of ordination must be understood differently. It is not a rite that sets certain persons apart for a unifying function; ecclesial unity is grounded elsewhere.

Christian Community

Scholars today are in general agreement that the NT churches reflect a multiplicity of structures.[115] Hans Küng calls attention to this variety when he states, "there are significant differences between the image of the Church which is adumbrated in Matthew and that in Luke, between the image of the Church in the gospel of St John and that in Ephesians and Colossians, between the image of the Church in Paul's four great epistles . . . and that in the pastoral epistles."[116] The structures were pluriform. Amidst this diversity, however, at least one common element can be identified.

While the structures of the early church were marked by diversity, all these emerging structures had in common a communal dimension. Arthur Gish suggests that most of the biblical images of the church fall under one of four main themes: 1) the people of God; 2) the new humanity; 3) the fellowship of believers; and 4) the body of Christ.[117] All these themes are communal in nature. Volf takes Matthew 18:20 as the biblical starting point for his understanding of the church,[118] and here, in the idea that where two or three are gathered in Christ's name He is present, we also see the communal dimension. Volf rightly calls attention to the idea that part of the ecclesiality of the church is that it is an assembly.[119] These approaches point to community as central to the ecclesiality of the church.

The way in which community is fundamental to the nature of the church leaves no room for office to be central to ecclesiality. This assertion is in contrast with the Catholic ecclesiology set forth by Vatican II

115. See, for example, "Ministry/BEM," §22.
116. Küng, *The Church*, 38.
117. Gish, *Living in Christian Community*, 21.
118. Volf, *After Our Likeness*, 136.
119. Ibid., 137.

which affirmed that bishops bring the presence of Christ to the people[120] and that, because they are Christ's representatives in a special way, only priests can officiate at the Lord's supper.[121] The Eucharist stands at the center of this ecclesiology, and because only priests can preside over the Eucharist, priests also are central. My assertion regarding the centrality of community precludes such a position for office holders. Communal relationships, not office, are central to the ecclesiality of the church.

I agree with BEM and Vatican II that the ordained and the community are interrelated. But I disagree regarding the nature of this relationship. *Lumen Gentium* states "the common priesthood of the faithful and the ministerial or hierarchical priesthood are . . . ordered one to another."[122] In this view, the two are related, but they are distinct. I hold that the two are related precisely because they are *not* distinct. Ordained individuals are related to the community not because they are merely ordered to community, but because they are of the same substance as the community. An internal relationship exists. Ordained individuals are not related to the community primarily through a certain position or function, but through a common sharing in a single priesthood grounded in the Holy Spirit.

Implications

If no special charisms are conveyed in the act of ordination, what then is the nature of this act? From the perspective of the congregation, ordination should be viewed as recognition and affirmation of a gift which has been bestowed upon an individual for the building up of the body. From the perspective of the one being ordained this rite should be viewed as a public acknowledgement of a gift that has been received and a public commitment to use this gift for the benefit of the body.

Based on the view of charisms set forth above, I would like to expand on Volf's view of ordination. I embrace most of Volf's description of ordination. He points out that ordination is a divine-human act which involves a public acknowledgment of a charism given by God and he argues that *"ordination is an act of the entire local church led by the Spirit of*

---

120. "*Lumen Gentium*," §21.

121. "*Presbyterorum Ordinis*," §2, §5, §6.

122. "*Lumen Gentium*," §10. Cf. "Ministry/BEM," §12.

God."[123] He also asserts that ordination is not necessarily appointment to a lifelong task. This is consistent with the view that charisms are diachronic. I want to go further, though, and call for an even broader understanding of ordination. If 1) ordination is the acknowledgment of the gifting of God for a *particular* ministry; 2) *all* Christians are given charisms to be used in some form of ministry; and 3) *all* charisms, not just some, when properly used, represent and serve the entire local congregation, then why not ordain each and every person as she or he is called to a particular ministry? Rather than limiting ordination to those who are paid to do ministry, we should truly abolish the clergy/laity distinction. I concur with Moltmann that "all the members of the messianic community have the gift of the Spirit and are therefore 'office-bearers.' There is no division between office bearers and the people. There is no division between the Spirit of the ministry and the free Spirit."[124] Therefore we should ordain *all* who would publicly acknowledge their calls to ministry in whatever form that might be. People should be ordained to their ministries of teaching Sunday school, running a business, raising children, and yes, leading a church.

Some have argued that baptism should be viewed as ordination to ministry, and this is correct in part. It is correct in that the rite of baptism calls and marks people for the service of Christ, but baptism does not give specificity to this call. This specificity comes as a person is gifted by the Spirit; it changes as the person's charisms change. In the NT, the act of baptism and the act of consecration for a particular ministry task are two separate events. Baptism is a one-time, general ordination, but a specific and repeatable ordination is appropriate as well. In my view, we must not conflate the two.

What should be the nature of church structures given this view of ordination? Structures in and of themselves are not bad. In fact, structure—formal or informal—is required for any social entity to exist. Order and leadership are needed for a body to thrive.[125] Gish points to the *dangers* of not having leadership when he states that a "lack of clearly defined structure and roles does not necessarily mean freedom. It can also mean the rule of the strong over the weak, the manipulation of the more

---

123. Volf, *After Our Likeness*, 29 (emphasis original).

124. Moltmann, *The Church in the Power of the Spirit*, 298.

125. One treatment of this can be found in Warkentin, 165.

committed by those who are less committed."[126] This view of ordination does not lead to a rejection of structure. What *is* ruled out is any type of structure that leads to domineering authority or a type of structure that is forced upon a community. Church structures that are focused wholly on serving the community must exist alongside the view of ordination proposed here. These structures must have the flexibility to allow for the free moving of the Spirit. In a manner consistent with the NT witness, a variety of structures can meet these criteria. What they all must have in common is an authorization by the local congregation. If a congregation supports the three-fold offices of bishop, presbyter, and deacon, then such a structure is acceptable. But to be consistent with the view of charisms for which I have argued, these offices would need to be viewed in functional terms, not in terms of ontological difference or difference of priority. These offices should be given to individuals who have received charisms from the Spirit, charisms that would allow them to minister well through office.

If a congregation chooses a structure marked by a lack of any formal office, such a structure is also acceptable, as long as charisms such as leadership, preaching, and teaching are encouraged and allowed to function within the congregation. Trying to force all members of a congregation to use these charisms, which are not given to everyone, would go against the nature of charisms. It would mean denying individuals the freedom to exercise the particular gifts they have been given.

If we take ordination to be an act of identification and affirmation of the ways in which God has gifted a person, then as a new charism emerges in a person (as will happen given the diachronic plurality of charisms), or as an existing charism is given a new ministry expression, this person should be ordained again. In Acts 13 we read about Paul and Barnabas being appointed for a specific work to which God had called them. There is a particularity to this episode. We get no indication that the laying on of hands in these verses was to be taken as appointment to a life-long calling. A person may find that he or she does in fact focus on a particular ministry for the majority of his or her life, in which case he or she would only be ordained once, but this is not intrinsically a one-time event as is the case with baptism. In contrast, BEM states, "in recognition of the God-given charism of ministry, ordination to any one of the

126. Gish, 205.

particular ordained ministries is never repeated."[127] This position fails to acknowledge that the God who freely gives charisms through the Holy Spirit is also free to take away these charisms and is free to grant new charisms at will. A charism given by the Holy Spirit *may* be granted for life—the Spirit is free to grant in this manner, but permanence is not an intrinsic characteristic of the charisms.

Ordination must no longer be held as a requirement for those who would administer the Lord's supper. Since 1) all believers are gifted by the Spirit; 2) all charisms are of one nature; and 3) all believers should be ordained, no particular charism or office uniquely qualifies a person to administer the bread and the wine. It might be wise for a community to draw upon individuals who are mature in their faith and who embody the fruit of the Spirit to lead the community in the breaking of the bread and the drinking of the wine. But such selection would be based on embodied faith rather than on charisms or office.

Given this view of ordination, what is the nature of authority in the congregation? Vatican II and BEM are right that those who have authority in the church should use it to serve and build up the church. I wish to go further, however. This type of authority cannot be exercised over a congregation, if by this one means imposing authority upon a congregation. Legitimate authority in the church is grounded in Christ and bestowed by the Holy Spirit—a claim which Vatican II and BEM documents support. But how does the Holy Spirit bestow this authority? Through community. The Holy Spirit does not bestow authority in a way that bypasses community. The whole community shares responsibility for this authority. In Matthew 18:18–19, Jesus gives his followers the responsibility to bind and loose (cf. Matt 16:19), that is, the responsibility to exercise authority. This responsibility is given to all members of the church. A leader in a church may exercise authority in a way that others in the church might not exercise authority, but this authority is granted by the Holy Spirit through the community. Ecclesial authority ultimately is grounded in Christ, but it is conveyed through the community.

---

127. "Ministry/BEM," §48.

SUMMARY

Theological constructs and ecclesial structures are to be shaped and re-shaped by the nature of the Trinity. Given the nature of the Trinity, the church should be a pneumatic community marked by relationality. The church should always be moving outside itself to be present with others. In order to be present, the church must be open to the world and must unilaterally give itself to the world. Ecclesial relationships and roles are to be marked by equality and non-domination in correspondence with the trinitarian relations. The whole ecclesial community is to be thus characterized, including its leaders. In correspondence to the Trinity, the church is at once diverse and united.

This simultaneous diversity and unity is realized through the charisms. The Holy Spirit universally distributes charisms to all believers, who work interdependently to build up the body of Christ. No part of the body is more important than the others and so the charisms are marked by equality, an equality reflective of the trinitarian relations. Believers are to use their charisms conjunctively to move outside themselves, to be open to the world.

In light of the nature of the charisms, ordination is a rite that is to be administered to *all* the people of God. This does not negate the importance of leadership in the church, but it does acknowledge the equal nature of all other charisms. Every Christian acts as a representative of Christ, and therefore every Christian participates in a priestly function. Thought the NT does not describe or prescribe the ordaining of all Christians (nor, as I have argued, does it describe or prescribe the ordaining of a priestly class), I arrive at the idea of universal ordination theologically via the nature of the charisms and the priestly presence of Christ in every believer.

As construed in light of the Trinity, the priesthood of all believers is a metaphor that illuminates the nature of the church. As a social entity marked by presence, equality, non-domination, unity, and diversity, it challenges many current ecclesial structures. As a union of believers, it points up the relational nature of the church. And as a ministerial body, it assigns to every believer a vital role in the work of God.

FOUR

Institutions of Postmodernity
and the Priesthood of All Believers

The royal priesthood is a social entity. Given that we find ourselves participating in a number of social entities simultaneously, how does the priesthood of all believers relate to the other social constructs that exist in our culture? In this chapter I will describe three social structures in postmodern culture and examine the relationship between these and the priesthood of all believers.

I use the framework of institutions for this discussion, first describing institutions from a sociological perspective, and then explaining how the royal priesthood is an institution. Next I look at three institutions in our hyper-modern culture: globalization, individualism, and *technique*. I conclude each of these three sections by looking at how the values of these cultural institutions might coincide or clash with the values of the royal priesthood.

INSTITUTIONS AS CLUSTERS OF MEANING AND VALUES

In sociological language, institutions are meaning-laden patterns that we use to structure our lives together. Robert Bellah and his colleagues describe institutions as "normative patterns embedded in and enforced by laws and mores (informal customs and practices)."[1] These patterns carry in them ideals and meanings.[2] They communicate the actions that are

---

1. Bellah, Madsen, Sullivan, Swidler, and Tipton, *The Good Society*, 10–11.
2. Ibid., 40.

expected of individuals and groups. Institutions shape the ways we relate to each other. They mediate our shared lives and they influence the focus of our attention.

Institutions can be formal or informal, obvious or subtle.[3] Our society is quite conscious of some institutions such as marriage. Marriage defines for us certain relational patterns and provides social and legal means for enforcing its standards. We are less conscious of other institutions. A handshake is a simple institution that communicates at least a minimal level of openness between two people. The refusal to shake an extended hand is understood as an abrupt rejection of the other person, and because of our social codes, such a refusal is seldom seen—we expect even political enemies to shake hands when they meet face to face.

Moral values are embedded in and communicated through institutions.[4] As we go through our days, our decisions and choices are connected to institutional values. When I take my child to school in the morning, I do not first carry out an internal debate regarding the nature of our educational system, the safety of this particular school, and the racial diversity of the classroom. These issues are all relevant to the institution of education, but my actions on most days are tied to a basic and strong value embedded in the institution: it is good for a child to get an education.

Classic liberalism has held that institutions ought to be value neutral. It holds that institutions should simply be mechanisms that allow individuals to carry out their choices.[5] But this position is naïve, blind to the realities of powers and structures. Bellah says that institutions are "never neutral but . . . always ethical and political, since institutions . . . live or die by ideas of right and wrong and conceptions of the good."[6] The question, then, is not whether or not a given institution has a moral dimension, but rather, what is the nature of an institution's morality. The values of Little League Baseball include teamwork and sportsmanship. Hatred and discrimination are values embedded in the institution of racism. All institutions communicate moral values.

---

3. Ibid., 10.

4. Ibid.

5. Ibid.

6. Ibid., 11–12.

Institutions have a norming dimension to them. They call for us to conform to the values embedded in them. They communicate what is expected and they provide sanctions, both positive and negative, for enforcing the norms. If I were to hold my child out of school, I would face social sanctions in the form of the disdain of my extended family and friends. I would also face legal sanctions because as a society we have decided that children must participate in this institution up to a certain age. Sanctions or social pressures can take a positive form as well. If I make sure that my child attends school and if I encourage my child to excel academically, the institution rewards me by giving me a bumper sticker that advertises to all that my child is an honor student (and therefore I have done well at meeting the institutional expectations). Institutions maintain their identities by punishing and rewarding those who come under their influence.

The norms of a given institution can change. They seldom change quickly, but the notion that they can change is a fundamental assumption of Bellah. His analysis of American culture shows the institutions we have today are not static. The possibility exists that they will change again in the future.

Although in popular parlance institutions and organizations are commonly viewed as synonymous, as used here the two must be distinguished. Organizations are concrete manifestations of institutions.[7] Microsoft is an example of an organization. It is also part of the institution of the corporation. The distinction is important because it determines the way in which one might challenge or seek to reform an organization like Microsoft. One approach would be to hold Microsoft accountable to the norms that our society has created for corporations; Microsoft has faced such challenges in recent years through the legal system. But a second, more fundamental challenge is also possible. One might challenge the very norms of the institution; that is, one might challenge the way we as a society have conceptualized corporations rather than just challenging the nature of a particular organization. Microsoft as an organization might do a good job of living by the standards of the corporation as institution, but if the institution itself is built on ethically shallow premises, then the institution itself must be changed. This would mean defining a revised value set for the institution and creating laws that reflect these values and

---

7. Ibid., 11.

standards. The organization can then be held to the re-shaped values and norms of the institution.

Institutions always have moral content, whether good, bad, or mixed. Each institution requires and assumes a value set in order to function. Democracy, for example, requires honesty to be the norm. In any democracy, some people will act dishonestly, but where corruption and deceit are widespread, democracy cannot thrive. Consumerism as an institution requires that material things be highly valued. Consumerism is premised on and promotes materialism. The institution pushes this value because materialism is essential for the survival of consumerism—if people do not highly value material goods, they cannot be persuaded to continue forward in a purchasing frenzy. The question, then, is not "are institutions moral?" but "what is the nature of this institution's morality?"

Americans tend to have a negative view of institutions because, Bellah claims, "individualistic Americans fear that institutions impinge on their freedom."[8] While Americans normally see institutions as being at odds with individualism, Bellah thinks that this is a misunderstanding of institutions. He holds that institutions are what *enable* individualism.[9] I would suggest, however, that individualism *itself* is an institution, and so the fear expressed as "freedom vs. institutions" is really an institutional conflict—a conflict between the institution of individualism (which values freedom) and other institutions. I will give extended attention below to individualism as an institution.

Institutions have an asymmetrical relationship with individuals. While individuals collectively form and sustain institutions, institutions "guide and sustain individual identity," they "give shape to collective and individual experience."[10] The power of the institution over the individual usually exceeds the power of the individual over the institution. Institutions arise out of human interactions, but they become forces

8. Ibid., 10. Later the authors claim that Americans expect institutions to serve the individual (p. 289). Are these contradictory claims? Do institutions impinge on our individualism or serve our individualism? I suggest that Americans want institutions to serve the individual but fear that the institutions might swallow up the individual. Understood in this way, the two claims are not necessarily contradictory. It is also possible that Americans simultaneously hold conflicting views of institutions. This would be consistent with the complex nature of many institutions. Our relationships with institutions are often ambivalent.

9. Ibid., 6.

10. Ibid., 40. See also p. 12.

not dependent upon any given individual. Individuals can bring about changes in the shape or nature of an institution, but these changes do not come easily.

This institutional view stands in contrast to rational choice theory. The latter holds that individuals act rationally and make choices that are in their own material interest. Bellah argues that individuals' choices are not made primarily on a rational basis but on the basis of institutional norms.[11] This means that an individual's identity is highly dependent on the institutions of society; it is not based simply on pursuing one's own best interests. Some of these societal institutions do indeed promote one's own short-term best interests as rational choice theory suggests, but other institutions promote the long-term good of the community.

Often Christians who have promoted the priesthood of all believers have cast their arguments in anti-hierarchical (anti-institutional) terms, so it might seem rather ironic that I have chosen to use an institutional framework to gain insight regarding the royal priesthood. However, with the understanding of institutions as set forth above, we can see that the real issue is not one of the priesthood of all believers versus the institutional church. The real issue is what the institution called "church" should look like. The participatory ecclesiology argued for in chapter three *is* an institutional form—it carries with it forming and norming values.

The church is one of multiple institutions that touch the lives of Christians. At times other institutions complement and reinforce the church, while at other times other institutions stand in conflict with the church. We shall now look at three powerful institutions in our postmodern culture: globalization, individualism, and *technique*. The thinking of several writers on each institution will be set forth, the values of each of these three institutions will be identified, and these values will be analyzed to discover how they might encourage or undercut the values of the royal priesthood.

GLOBALIZATION

Globalization is perhaps most commonly understood in economic terms: a car today might be produced by a company headquartered in one country and assembled in a second country using parts made in a third

11. Ibid., 290.

country. This economic understanding is indeed one aspect of globalization, but globalization is an institution with cultural, political, and moral features as well.

This section discusses how three different thinkers understand globalization. Michael Budde analyzes the institution of globalization by looking at what he labels "global culture industries." Anthony Giddens sees globalization as a runaway economic force that must be brought to heel. Bob Goudzwaard argues that different types of globalization are available to us. After setting forth these three perspectives I will look at how globalization relates to the priesthood of all believers.

Michael Budde and Global Culture Industries

Michael Budde frames his discussion of globalization by outlining three characteristics of postmodern culture. First, postmodernity is unlike any culture that has existed before because people living in this culture are constantly exposed to mediated messages and experiences. Second, postmodernity is characterized by fragmentation. The links between symbols and their referents have been severed and so we have no context for understanding symbols and we lack resources for establishing the relationships between various symbols. Third, postmodernity holds high a social ideal that has never held such a place of prominence before: the social ideal of consumption.[12]

According to Budde, this cultural environment has become dominated by global culture industries.[13] Global culture industries are composed of for-profit business firms that operate globally. While earlier global industries involved sectors such as automobiles and electronics, these global *culture* industries are focused on media, information, communications, and entertainment.[14] This category includes mass communications, but it is even broader; it includes "those industries that act as vectors, conveyors, or infrastructural requisites for cultural enterprises."[15] Disney and Time Warner are examples of such companies. They are far-flung enterprises that go well beyond the production of movies or magazines.

---

12. Budde, *The (Magic) Kingdom of God*, 36–37.

13. Ibid., 14.

14. Ibid., 28.

15. Ibid.

They have numerous subsidiaries that encompass a wide range of businesses (e.g., selling CDs, merchandising through fast food chains, running theme parks). Budde argues that these industries require a certain culture to flourish, and therefore they work to create and sustain such a culture.

In congruence with the description above regarding the nature of institutions, global culture industries seek to promote a set of normative patterns that form meanings and identity. They "struggle to define or affect self- and group perceptions in ways congenial to profitability, regularity, and social control."[16] Budde calls this struggle the "politics of identity" and sees transnational firms as major players in the competition to form people's identities.[17] This struggle to shape identity is not limited to national boundaries, but rather, fluidly crosses these and other boundaries as the institution seeks to develop and expand markets.

Consumption is a significant societal good in this value system because of its role in capitalism, a core component of this institution. At one time, production was the primary challenge of capitalism. But today the bigger problem is how to create a level of consumption that can keep up with the productive capacity. Greater levels of consumption are required for the current phase of capitalism to work.[18] Therefore, one of the tasks of the global culture industries is to create demand for products and services in order to ensure a lively rate of consumption. Consumption will lead to further economic expansion and the economic benefits will accrue to all, so the argument goes. Budde highlights this view in a clever way when he states, "reversing St. Paul's dictum ('anyone unwilling to work should not eat', 2 Thes 3:10), the postfordist economy dictates that if people will not eat (and drink and buy compact discs and travel abroad and purchase the latest in fashions, home appliances, and the like) in sufficient volume, then no one will work."[19] The institution communicates that consumption is something in which all should actively participate.

Budde identifies advertising and marketing as the most central global culture industry because advertising and marketing today extend

16. Ibid., 18.
17. Ibid.
18. Ibid., 37.
19. Ibid., 26.

into virtually every other realm of cultural production.[20] It is the job of this industry to create the desire that will lead to the level of consumption necessary for the capitalist system to roll forward. The advertising/ marketing industry has sought to portray itself as providing a service for consumers. In this view, consumers are presented with various options and then are free to make a rational choice based on characteristics such as price, quality, and a product's features. Budde views the industry as much more sinister. He believes that "marketing and advertising in a postmodern context represent techniques of power in the contemporary world—that is, a web of observation, surveillance, and attempts at behavior modification that stretches from the global culture industries down to the isolated consumer/individual."[21] He believes that in spite of what the industry might say, it does *not* view consumers as rational choice-makers. The advertising and marketing industry views consumers as open to manipulation. In seeking to manipulate individuals to consume more products, advertising and marketing are, thus, a center of power. The industry uses its power not only to castigate or punish those who do not abide by its norms, but also to create and re-create the norms themselves. Power is wielded negatively in ways like the creation of social sanctions against people whose way of dressing does not conform to its norms or who do not own certain products. The industry exercises power positively by "generating new knowledge, new behaviors, new norms and expectations, and new social conceptions of truth."[22]

Television is another powerful factor within the global culture industries. Budde gives special attention to television because he believes that television has had a huge transformative impact on our culture as a whole and on our individual lives.[23] Television is such a powerful industry because of the way it disseminates and validates "common stories, symbols, sounds, pictures, information, 'news', values, frames of reality, and social archetypes."[24] In this description we see again the characteristics of an institution: it transmits morals and meanings, and patterns relationships.

20. Ibid., 34.
21. Ibid., 39.
22. Ibid., 40.
23. Ibid., 71.
24. Ibid.

Budde's critique of television is not focused on programming content.[25] His focus is on the medium itself. He argues that the rapidly changing pictures, the editing conventions, and the easily decodable images all contribute to an institution that has emotional, psychological, and physiological power.[26] This power forms us in ways that conflict with the gospel. The solution is not to replace bad content with good content:

> The church does not gain if the 20 to 30 hours of TV viewing each week changes from cops and sleaze to socially uplifting messages—it wouldn't gain from 20 to 30 hours of TV viewing of religious programming for that matter. With so many hours of human existence in the thrall of commercial culture industries, with human attention surrounded by barkers and enticers and noisemakers, the quiet but single-minded call to the gospel cannot be heard.[27]

The forming power of television competes with the forming power of the gospel. Television not only takes away time that is needed for the life-long process of spiritual formation, but it also creates a mindset that is unwilling to engage in long-term processes.

Context is required to understand language, symbols, and events, but television "is notoriously poor at providing any context or framing outside itself."[28] Television offers snippets of information without historical context or communal memory to make sense of it. The lack of context makes it difficult for people to make meaningful connections between various events and images. People get bits and pieces of information, but it is fragmented and must remain so because people do not have anything to guide them in putting the puzzle pieces together. To the extent that Christians get their primary formation from television, their formation will contain large gaps of understanding and disjointed images. It is only from within the context of the Christian community that "well-developed schemas" regarding the gospel can be handed on.[29]

25. Ibid., 95–96.

26. Ibid., 75–76, 78.

27. Ibid., 96.

28. Ibid., 85. Cf. Bellah, Madsen, Sullivan, Swidler, and Tipton, *The Good Society*, 38: "Much of the information coming to us in newspapers or on the television news remains incomprehensible because we lack a sense of institutional context that would make it seem human."

29. Budde, *The (Magic) Kingdom of God*, 86.

Budde's purpose in undertaking this cultural analysis is to show how the church is impacted by the current culture. He argues that the ways in which the global culture industries seek to shape people—both the processes and the goals—are in direct conflict with the processes and goals of Christian formation.

This analysis points up several of the ethical values embedded in globalization. Budde explicitly states that consumption is a value of globalization. Consumption is required to keep the system running and so needs are created in order to fuel consumption. Budde implicitly shows that short-term results are another value of this institution. Television is one way this value is promoted. The images flashed at us by television lack connections to the past or the future—all that matters is the present. The emphasis is on one's immediate gratification. Time is another value present here. Global culture industries value our time and are not content with just a small portion of it; they seek to monopolize it.

Anthony Giddens: Bringing Our Runaway World to Heel

Globalization is a runaway force that is profoundly restructuring our lives, a force we cannot completely control, but one we must bring to heel.[30] This is the perspective set forth by Anthony Giddens.

In contrast to Budde, Giddens holds a fairly positive view of globalization. While he states, "we can see cause for optimism and pessimism in about equal measure,"[31] his view is definitely tilted toward optimism. He acknowledges that globalization has a dark side, but he believes that globalization, if channeled properly, can be a positive force,[32] and he is optimistic about humanity's ability to channel globalization in a positive way.[33]

Several basic values shape Giddens's view of globalization, including cosmopolitanism, democracy, and "pure" relationships. In response to the forces of globalization, some people move towards fundamentalism while others move towards cosmopolitanism. Giddens promotes the latter. He speaks approvingly of "cosmopolitan values" and "cosmopolitan

---

30. Giddens, *Runaway World*, 4–5.

31. Ibid., 81.

32. Ibid., xvi.

33. Ibid., 19 and passim.

morality,"[34] although he does not explicitly articulate their substance. He implies that cosmopolitanism, in contrast to fundamentalism, is characterized by tolerance and dialogue.[35] He links these characteristics with "values of a universal kind,"[36] and exhorts us to defend actively these values, although again he does not state what "values of a universal kind" he might be referring to, nor how one might argue for their universality. Giddens seems to take it as self-evident that cosmopolitanism is a good thing, and so, to the extent that globalization promotes it, globalization is a good thing too.

Globalization, too, has been an important force in the spread of democracy, which, like cosmopolitism, Giddens views in a positive way.[37] Giddens acknowledges that in some ways globalization works *against* democracy. It can pull power away from local communities. On the other hand, claims Giddens, globalization "also pushes downward, creating new pressures for local autonomy."[38] Global communications have been one of the key reasons for the rapid spread of democracy that has occurred in the last forty years.[39] Giddens evaluates cultural shifts based on the extent to which they promote democracy.

Globalization is also positively reshaping many of our traditional relationships. Giddens argues that in marriage relationships, in parent-child relationships, and in friendships a shift is taking place. Traditionally, these relationships have been strongly shaped by extended family and social webs.[40] Today these are becoming more "pure relationships," a term Giddens uses to refer to relationships that are based on emotional communication, active trust, and disclosure.[41] In drawing parallels between pure relationships and democracy, Giddens claims such relationships involve a "democracy of emotions,"[42] something not characteristic of traditional relationships. He contends that the democratization of the family is a key force in promoting political democracy and economic development. For

34. Ibid., 50.
35. Ibid.
36. Ibid.
37. Ibid., 5.
38. Ibid., 13.
39. Ibid., 68.
40. Ibid.
41. Ibid., 61.
42. Ibid., 63.

Giddens, pure relationships serve as yet another validating criterion for globalization.

In seeking to understand the shifts that are related to globalization, Giddens uses the helpful phrase "shell institutions" to refer to "institutions that appear the same as they used to be from the outside, and carry the same names, but inside have become quite different."[43] Examples of shell institutions include marriage, work, nature, and nation. The outer shell of the institution remains the same, but the inner content—the images and meanings contained in the shell—has changed dramatically.[44] Given the ways in which our world has changed, these institutions are no longer able to perform the tasks once expected of them.[45]

Giddens's analysis of globalization is provocative at several points. First, Giddens argues that nations remain much more powerful than corporations.[46] He points out that nations continue to control territory, establish laws, and hold military power, things that corporations do not do. He believes that those who claim that corporations run the world have greatly exaggerated the situation.[47] Second, Giddens argues that economic inequalities are diminishing as a result of globalization. He acknowledges that in some places inequalities have increased, but overall "the evidences suggests that these factors [market competition and free trade that come with globalization] favour economic growth and on balance tend to cause inequalities to lessen, not intensify."[48] Third, Giddens holds that globalization *increases* cultural diversity. The idea that globalization brings about cultural standardization "is a relatively superficial cultural veneer; a more profound effect of globalisation is to produce greater local cultural di-

43. Ibid., 18. Zygmunt Bauman refers to the same phenomenon as "zombie institutions" (*Liquid Modernity*, 6).

44. Family, for example, in the past was understood in terms of a relational network much broader than the nuclear family, and the concept of family was tied to the institution of marriage. Today, however, the couple, not the broader network of relatives, is at the center of what it means to be a family. And unmarried couples, with or without children, are more and more considered to be families. While the concept of family still exists, the institution of family has been emptied of many previous meanings. Thus in Giddens' view, family has become a shell institution. Giddens, *Runaway World*, 58.

45. Ibid., 19.

46. Ibid., xxv.

47. Ibid.

48. Ibid., xxviii.

versity, not homogeneity."[49] Numerous voices speaking on globalization would contest these claims.[50]

The way in which Giddens views globalization certainly qualifies it as an institution. He makes it clear that the patterns of globalization can and should carry moral values. Globalization has indeed shaped the ways we relate to each other. He recognizes the challenge of changing or directing globalization because, like all institutions, it will not be changed easily. Yet he also recognizes that institutions can be changed and he is optimistic that globalization can be directed in ways that enhance our lives.

Bob Goudzwaard: Wishful Thinking About Globalization

Is globalization good or bad? It all depends, according to Bob Goudzwaard.[51] Goudzwaard argues that globalization comes in different forms. He seeks to identify the form of globalization that dominates our society today and he suggests ways to promote a "good" globalization.

Goudzwaard begins with the position that God has given us both the created world and the creations that have arisen from human action in history.[52] Science, technology and economics fall into this latter category. Goudzwaard believes that these are given to us by God, so we must not view them as intrinsically evil.[53] Rather, we must evaluate individual aspects or actions of globalization and judge each one separately. He calls for "selective normative criteria" to be used in this process.[54] This will allow for precise rather than sweeping judgments.

Goudzwaard views the form of globalization that dominates our world today as the process by which technology, finance, and economic practice shape our societies.[55] International finance is the most powerful

49. Ibid., xxiv.

50. See, for example, Korten, *When Corporations Rule the World*; Budde, *The (Magic) Kingdom of God*; Wiarda, "Has the 'End of History' Arrived?"

51. Goudzwaard, *Globalization and the Kingdom of God*, 20.

52. Goudzwaard draws explicitly on his Reformed tradition in developing this position. Ibid.

53. Budde refers to this position as "sacramental liberalism." He argues that such a position is highly reductive and fails to see the connections involved in globalization. He also argues that just because good uses can be imagined, this doesn't mean that they are likely. See Budde, *The (Magic) Kingdom of God*, 98–100.

54. Goudzwaard, *Globalization and the Kingdom of God*, 21.

55. Ibid., 19.

force within globalization. Goudzwaard describes one view that sees the financial system as mechanistic. This leads to an abdication of responsibility, for if the machine produces outcomes automatically, then we are not responsible for those outcomes.[56] He rejects this view and argues that we do in fact have a responsibility to address the current structure, which contains unjust values because it puts poorer countries at a disadvantage from the start and keeps them in that position.[57] The current economic structure is *not* mechanistic and the outcomes are *not* inevitable.

Goudzwaard's view is that globalization is not inherently evil. He is arguing here that *this particular* economic structure is unjust. He can imagine a form of globalization that does *not* have injustice structured into it.

Perhaps the greatest contribution Goudzwaard makes to the discussion of globalization is his treatment of competition. He identifies competition as a hallmark of capitalism and he laments that the competitive spirit spawned by capitalism has spread far beyond economics.[58] It now shapes everything from education to orchestras, from hospitals to governments. He thinks this influence of capitalism on other spheres of life is a boundary violation. The competitive rules of capitalism should not be allowed to permeate spheres such as family and government.[59] The broad repercussions of competition are what Goudzwaard refers to as the *breadth* of competition's structural impact.[60]

There is also a *depth* to the structural impact of competition.[61] Economic competition no longer just seeks to meet existing demands. Competition now seeks to create new demands. This structural shift has a cultural impact as the cycle of new demands-new developments spins. This "demand-management is . . . becoming one of the deep structural characteristics of the entire Western economy."[62]

56. Ibid., 25.

57. Ibid., 23–24.

58. Ibid., 29.

59. Ibid., 31.

60. Ibid., 30.

61. Ibid., 31. For a fully developed perspective on how various spheres should be bounded, see Walzer, *Spheres of Justice.*

62. Goudzwaard, *Globalization and the Kingdom of God,* 32.

Goudzwaard identifies three significant risks associated with economic competition.[63] First, the poor are put at risk. To meet the demands created by capitalism, the system uses resources that are then not available to countries and people living in poverty. A second risk is the degradation of the environment. The patterns of production and consumption, which are encouraged by competition, cause severe environmental damage. The third risk is to all of humanity, poor and rich alike. The risk here is that we will come to believe that the present competitive economic system is the only alternative. This is the risk of hypnosis.

In Goudzwaard's view, the competitive economic system *has* in fact hypnotized us and so we now *do* believe that no other alternatives to the current system exist. Competition is taken to be a universal law that naturally dictates how every aspect of society should function.[64] For us to choose a good type of globalization, we must escape from this hypnosis. Although Goudzwaard paints a frightful picture of our current dilemma, he is optimistic about our chances of overcoming our hypnotic state.

We must reject a fatalistic view of the system and embrace a responsible, aware view that sees real potential for change and for choosing different options. With this view, we can move towards a "good" type of globalization. Goudzwaard repeatedly calls on us to give up "childish" views and to adopt "mature" views.[65] He sees this as the way to escape the hypnosis that keeps us trapped in the current form of globalization.

Globalization and the Priesthood of All Believers

How does the institution of globalization relate to the institution of the priesthood of all believers? At some points the two institutions are complementary. Giddens has pointed to democracy as a core value of globalization. Democracy has a participatory aspect to it, and participation is a core value of the royal priesthood. In both institutions, all members have the opportunity for expression, but not all forms of democracy guarantee that the minority voices will be fully listened to and honored in the way they must be within the priesthood of all believers.

---

63. Ibid., 32–33.
64. Ibid., 35.
65. Ibid., 36–39, 42, 44.

The "pure relationships" that Giddens values can also complement the values of the royal priesthood. Within the church, relationships *should* involve the emotional connection, active trust, and transparency of Giddens' pure relationships. However, for Christians these characteristics must remain attached to the social web of the royal priesthood. The relationships of those in the royal priesthood are also to include commitment to the other, obligation based on covenant, and sacrificial service. A therapeutic relational model is inadequate on its own.

The cosmopolitanism that Giddens advocates, understood as tolerance, certainly has a place within the priesthood of all believers. The theological understanding of the charisms set forth in chapter three calls for Christians to celebrate differences in giftings. This affirmation of differences is to extend beyond the church as well.[66] But once again, the correspondence between the values of these two institutions is partial. The cosmopolitanism of postmodernity pushes not just toleration, but acceptance of all views. Those in the body of Christ are to respect all others, and yet Christians are not free to indiscriminately accept all other viewpoints.

Goudzwaard has focused in on competition as a core value of globalization. As a core value, it must be seen as fundamentally at odds with the values of the body of Christ. The nature of the charisms calls for cooperation, not competition. Competition implies that someone wins and others lose. For Christians to pursue winning at the expense of others would violate the self-giving and mutuality that characterize the Trinity and that therefore are to mark the royal priesthood. Competition also has within it the impulse for monopoly and monopoly results in domination. Again, we have a clash with the trinitarian characteristic of non-domination that marks the royal priesthood. On a shallow level Christians are free to compete, for example, in a soccer game or for a job. But competition cannot be a core value. It cannot drive our primary motivations nor shape our identities. Our relational patterns and our lifestyle habits are to be formed with the interests of others in mind. We are not to compete on behalf of our own best interests; rather, we are to work for the good of all.

The fact that those in the royal priesthood are to look also to the interests of others puts this institution in conflict with the postmodern value of consumption, which Budde highlighted. The forms of consump-

---

66. For a full discussion of how this should be manifest in the body of Christ and how it should extend into culture, see Yoder, *Body Politics*, 47–60.

tion pushed by our culture are connected to the deprivation of the poor around the world. As Goudzwaard notes, financial and natural resources that go towards culturally cultivated patterns of consumption are unavailable for meeting the basic needs of the non-rich. Consumption poses an additional problem: it promises to meet our deepest longings. It claims to be the well of living water that will not run dry. Those in the royal priesthood reject such a claim. Christ alone is this well. We have hope of satisfaction not through consuming but through our connection to Christ.

Budde has pointed out that postmodern culture places a high value on immediate gratification. This is problematic for Christians because the process of being formed as a priesthood and as priests is not a short-term one. The training and formation required of those in the royal priesthood is life-long. It cannot be accomplished in a matter of hours or days. Christian spiritual formation requires attentiveness to the Spirit over a long period of time—indeed, it requires a lifetime.

While points of congruence can be found, at many points the institutions of globalization and the royal priesthood clash. Without an awareness of the conflicting institutional values, Christians will end up more formed by the power of globalization than they are by their identity as a royal priesthood. Christians must allow the institutional values of the royal priesthood to be primary in patterning their relationships and ways of living.

INDIVIDUALISM

Individualism is a second major institution of postmodernity. Conceptualizing individualism as an institution points to the fact that individualism patterns our ways of living, and the patterns it sets forth are value-laden. In this section I shall show how three different thinkers analyze individualism and I shall then bring to light the values embedded in this institution and relate them to the priesthood of all believers.

Robert Bellah on the Rise of Individualism in America

The common vocabulary that is shared in the US is that of individualism, according to Robert Bellah and his colleagues.[67] While individual-

---

67. Bellah et al., *Habits of the Heart,* 20.

ism brings with it a certain type of liberation, Bellah is concerned with the down side of individualism. He is convinced that the language of individualism does not provide an adequate means for talking about and addressing the moral dilemmas we face today as a society. In order to address the problem, we must first understand the situation.

Bellah describes four different types of individualism that have been present in the United States. The first is what he calls biblical individualism. Prominent in the United States during the seventeenth and eighteenth centuries, this is a way of conceptualizing individualism in terms of freedom *for* something, not freedom *from* something.[68] A second type of individualism is civic or republican individualism. This type of individualism focuses on the rights of citizens. It does not conceive of freedom strictly in terms of individual benefit, but freedom no longer has a moral obligation attached to it—it is no longer seen as freedom *for*.[69] Utilitarian individualism is a third type, a type which Bellah argues is at the heart of our culture today. This view of individualism holds that what is good for society will automatically come forth when people pursue that which is in their own best interests.[70] The fourth type, also central to our culture today, is expressive individualism. With expressive individualism the focus is on a person celebrating oneself and being emotionally and sensually connected with others and with creation, in a way detached from one's job or civic duties.[71] Utilitarian individualism dominates the public sphere while expressive individualism dominates the private sphere. The two types are in conflict and thus significant tension exists between our private and public lives.[72]

The private sphere has come to emphasize the importance of defining oneself, a self that is no longer defined in terms of social and cultural traditions.[73] Leaving home has become a key step in this process of self-definition.[74] Children are raised with the assumption that they are to become independent—they are to leave home and make it on their

68. Ibid., 29.
69. Ibid., 31.
70. Ibid., 33.
71. Ibid., 34–35.
72. Ibid., 45–46.
73. Ibid., 55.
74. Ibid., 56–62.

own. The goal is to produce self-sufficient individuals. Religious choice is also part of this process of self-definition.[75] We have come to expect individuals to decide for themselves what religion or church to embrace. People are expected to make such choices autonomously, free from the influence of family or tradition. But this expectation contains an irony, which Bellah notes: "just where we think we are most free, we are most coerced by the dominant beliefs of our own culture. For it is a powerful cultural fiction that we not only can, but must, make up our deepest beliefs in the isolation of our private selves."[76] The autonomy of religious choice is a stated cultural value, but it doesn't adequately account for how such choices are actually made. The changed relationship between the self and work is connected to this issue of self-definition. Work is no longer viewed in terms of a "calling," but in terms of an activity that is separate from one's self, an activity in which one engages based on a calculation of the benefits it will deliver to the individual.[77] This move separates work from one's identity. Work is not considered part of one's self-definition.

Individualism in the private sphere is evidenced in the rise of what Bellah terms "lifestyle enclaves." These are social groups based on commonalities such as leisure activities or consumption patterns. People join such enclaves because of the way these enclaves allow individuals to pursue their private lifestyles. Lifestyle enclaves on the surface look like communities, but whereas communities celebrate interdependence, lifestyle enclaves celebrate "the narcissism of similarity."[78] Lifestyle enclaves now provide a primary source—albeit a shallow one—for developing one's individual identity.[79]

Our conceptions of relationships have been impacted by individualism. Marriage was once rooted firmly in social patterns and expectations, but marriage has been re-conceptualized in terms of self-fulfillment.[80] Love is seen as the basis for marriage and this creates tensions because, while love is seen as integral to expressive individualism, love also implies

75. Ibid., 62–65.

76. Ibid., 65.

77. Ibid., 69. Bellah notes that the idea of calling was present in the biblical and civic forms of individualism, forms which have now faded away in our culture (66).

78. Ibid., 73.

79. Ibid., 75.

80. Ibid., 85–89.

mutuality and interdependence.[81] To put it another way, love contains elements of both freedom and obligation and these elements pull in opposite directions. Friendships have been impacted by the rise of individualism. Earlier conceptions of friendship included a common commitment to the good, but this external common commitment is no longer seen as integral to a friendship.[82] Friendships are now patterned after a therapeutic model. Relationships are seen as a means to one's own ends, not as the means to a common end. Therefore our friendships now contain a cost-benefit calculation in terms of the psychic benefits.[83]

The public sphere has also been impacted by the rise of individualism. Bellah points out that Americans have always been "joiners." They are expected to get involved with social groups of their own choosing.[84] The nature of this involvement has changed, however. In the eighteenth and nineteenth centuries, such civic involvement was characterized by a commitment to the public good, a commitment that carried with it a moral language for discussing the public good. Civic involvement is now seen in terms of the benefit for the individual.[85] The concept of citizenship has been transformed by individualism. Whereas a good citizen was once understood to be a person who joined others in working for the common good, now a good citizen is one who simply obeys the laws.[86] A concern for others is not central to good citizenship now. The relation between the public sphere and religion is another area that has undergone change. Bellah longs for the church to be involved in the public discourse in America and points to biblical motifs that indicate that the church *should* be involved in this discourse. However, in the US, religion has been confined more and more to the private sphere. Bellah argues, "most Americans see religion as something individual, prior to any organizational involvement."[87] Religion is seen as serving the expressive individual, not the common good.

81. Ibid., 93.
82. Ibid., 115.
83. Ibid., 121–23, 127, and 134.
84. Ibid., 167.
85. Ibid., 177–78.
86. Ibid., 181.
87. Ibid., 226.

In summary, Bellah argues effectively that individualism has colored all aspects of American life, from the personal level to the societal level. Two types of individualism predominate today: utilitarian individualism and expressive individualism. These two types shape how we conceptualize both private and public life. While they are often at odds, these two types have at least one commonality: they are not concerned with the public good.[88] Although our society is more integrated than ever economically and technically, it remains

> a society in which the individual can only rarely and with difficulty understand himself and his activities as interrelated in morally meaningful ways with those of other, different Americans. Instead of directing cultural and individual energies toward relating the self to its larger context, the culture of manager [utilitarian individualism] and therapist [expressive individualism] urges a strenuous effort to make of our particular segment of life a small world of its own.[89]

Individualism positions us to define our personal and public lives solely in terms of our own interests.

These two dominant types of individualism point to several underlying values in our culture. Both types privilege the individual over the community. What is good for the individual is the highest good. Success is the primary value of utilitarian individualism. Those things that contribute to an individual's success are assigned a high worth. Positive emotional feelings are the primary value of expressive individualism. This is a therapeutic type that holds up the serenity and happiness of the individual as the highest good.

How might these values relate to the royal priesthood? We could easily jump to the assumption that the values embedded in the institution of individualism as described by Bellah are in fundamental conflict with the values embedded in the royal priesthood. Is this in fact the case? Before taking up this question, I will consider two other authors' perspectives on individualism in our culture.

---

88. Bellah's analysis of individualism is the content of his work that is of specific relevance to my discussion. Although I do not deal with it, he also proposes ways to overcome this individualism. In short, his solution is for individuals to re-attach to social and cultural contexts. This will contribute to the development of the type of character that is required to move people beyond themselves to seek the common good.

89. Bellah, *Habits of the Heart*, 50.

Robert Putnam and Social Capital

"We have been pulled apart from one another and from our communities over the last third of the century," claims Robert Putnam.[90] The decline of community has been accompanied by a corresponding rise of individualism. Putnam thoroughly documents *that* this has happened and seeks to understand *why* this has happened.

Social capital is the concept Putnam uses for his analysis. Social capital refers to "networks of relationships that weave individuals into groups and communities."[91] Social capital is a way of talking about the bonds of trust and understanding between people.

At the heart of social capital is the principle of reciprocity.[92] This reciprocity is not contractual in nature; it does not include the idea of equitable exchange. Rather, it is a generalized reciprocity. One does not expect an immediate benefit from watering a neighbor's plants while they are out of town, or taking one's turn teaching Sunday school, but these actions are accompanied by a loose expectation that down the road, in some form, the favor will be returned. One does not necessarily expect the favor to be returned by the same person and in the same way. This generalized reciprocity is a community asset. It benefits not only those within a particular relationship or network but has spillover benefits for bystanders as well.[93]

Putnam describes two types of social capital: bonding and bridging.[94] Bonding social capital links together people who are similar. It provides strong links within social or ethnic groups. Bridging social capital creates links between people from diverse social and cultural settings. Whereas bonding social capital is exclusive and inward looking, bridging social capital is inclusive and outward oriented. Both types of social capital are needed for a healthy society, according to Putnam.[95]

Social capital in our society has been declining, and the evidence of this decline is widespread. This decline can be seen in the area of political participation. The percentage of Americans who vote in presidential

90. Putnam, *Bowling Alone*, 27.

91. Putnam and Feldstein, *Better Together*, 1.

92. Putnam, *Bowling Alone*, 134.

93. Ibid., 136. Putnam and Feldstein, *Better Together*, 2.

94. Putnam, *Bowling Alone*, 22–23, Putnam and Feldstein, *Better Together*, 2–3.

95. Putnam and Feldstein, *Better Together*, 2.

elections has gradually declined for decades.[96] The number of political organizations in our country has actually been on the increase,[97] but this increase does not reflect an increase in participation by citizens. In fact, participation has dropped dramatically.[98] Americans remain reasonably well informed about politics, but they are less and less likely to actively participate.[99] Political participation produces less social capital than it once did.

Civic participation, as well, has declined markedly. Putnam looks at three forms of civic organizations: community based, church based, and work based. As in the political area, the number of civic organizations has increased significantly, but participation has decreased by more than fifty percent in the last several decades.[100] For many, membership now means simply supporting an organization financially. It does not assume active participation beyond this. The members of many of these organizations never actually meet each other. This drop in active civic involvement means that fewer networks of relationships are being fostered by such involvement.

What role do churches play in producing social capital? Putnam suggests, "faith communities in which people worship together are arguably the single most important repository of social capital in America."[101] People who are shaped by religious communities are more likely to be involved in other forms of civic activities. Polls show that Americans' personal levels of religious commitment have stayed relatively stable over the last few decades.[102] At the same time, however, church attendance has been declining for forty years.[103] Religion in America has become more privatized and less connected to religious communities. Religion continues to play a major role in our culture, but its production of social capital has diminished. This trend means that religion does not counter-

---

96. Putnam, *Bowling Alone*, 32–33. The high voter turnout for the 2004 presidential election contrasts with this trend. It will be interesting to see if this marks a reversal of the trend or a one-time exception.

97. Ibid., 38.

98. Statistics that support this claim can be found in ibid., 45.

99. Ibid., 46.

100. Ibid., 49, 61. Also, see chart on p. 54.

101. Ibid., 66.

102. Ibid., 69.

103. Ibid., 71.

balance the decline in social capital being produced by political and civic involvement.

To what extent does the workplace contribute to social capital? The decline in union membership over the last fifty years points to the weakening of workplace bonds.[104] Initially, this decline was accompanied by a rise in membership in professional organizations, a rise that reflected an economic re-organization. But over the last twenty years membership in professional organizations has declined as well.[105] Work-related organizations are producing a reduced amount of social capital, but what about workplace relationships that are not embedded in official organizations? These do not appear to be significant sources of social capital either. After analyzing these workplace relationships, Putnam concludes that the "structural changes in the workplace—shorter job tenure, more part-time and temporary jobs, and even independent consultancy—inhibit workplace-based social ties."[106] The decline in social capital found in other parts of society is not made up in the workplace.

In addition to looking at these more structured forms of connecting, Putnam looks at the informal ways we connect with each other. These are the ways in everyday life that we interact with friends and neighbors. Going to the movies, having friends over for dinner, and attending sporting events are examples of informal ways of connecting. Putnam analyzes an array of data on how we relate informally and concludes that today we are spending significantly less time together than in the past:

> We spend less time in conversation over meals, we exchange visits less often, we engage less often in leisure activities that encourage casual social interaction, we spend more time watching . . . and less time doing. We know our neighbors less well, and we see old friends less often. In short, it is not merely "do good" civic activities that engage us less, but also informal connecting.[107]

It is not just political and civic participation that has declined. People also spend less time together in informal situations, contributing further to the decline in social capital.

---

104. Ibid., 81.
105. Ibid., 84.
106. Ibid., 90.
107. Ibid., 115.

Why has social capital been declining over the last thirty years? While Putnam's observations regarding what is going in on our society are certainly helpful, his probing into the *reasons* for these changes are even more helpful. Putnam looks at the way four different factors contribute to the decline of social capital. Careful analysis of Putnam's first two factors—1) time and money, and 2) mobility and sprawl—shows a certain contribution to the decline of social capital, but surprisingly, the data show that neither of these factors are primary causes. Putnam documents that they impact social capital in only a minor way.[108]

A third factor, however, demonstrates a more marked impact. Putnam considers the significance of technology and mass media, noting two changes in the ways we get our news and entertainment. First, options are more individualized. Whereas a century ago one would need to go to the symphony with many other people and listen to selections that may or may not have been one's primary preference, now each individual is able to listen to precisely what he or she wants to hear.[109] Second, technology has moved entertainment more and more into the privacy of our homes. The way in which we partake of entertainment is more isolated than it was a century ago.[110]

Putnam further addresses the role of the internet in the development of social cohesion. In his work with Lewis Feldstein, he concludes that the internet does *not* build communities that produce any significant amount of social capital.[111] Email can supplement relationships that have been formed face-to-face, but it does little to create or develop relationships. Putnam and Feldstein state, "alloys of face-to-face and e-based ties can sustain social capital. By contrast, building trust and goodwill is not easy in the largely anonymous, easy-in, easy-out, surf-by world of pure cyberspace."[112] The internet has not existed long enough to be the main cause of the decline in social capital that began thirty years ago, but it has been around long enough to conclude that it does not counter the decline.

---

108. Ibid.

109. Ibid., 216.

110. Ibid., 217.

111. Putnam and Feldstein, *Better Together*.

112. Ibid., 235.

Television, on the other hand, has been a crucial factor in the decline of social capital. Television has drawn people into the home and away from leisure activities outside the home.[113] This isolating effect is compounded by the fact that, while television has drawn people into their homes, it has not built up relationships within these homes. In fact, it has had the opposite effect.[114] Putnam establishes that there is a correlation between watching television and civic disengagement. He further argues that television is in fact a *causal* factor in civic disengagement.[115] Television watching uses up time that could be spent in civic-strengthening endeavors, television produces a lethargic and passive mindset, and programming content undermines the motivations that contribute to social capital.[116]

Putnam argues that generational changes constitute a second prime reason for civic disengagement. Research has shown that as individuals move through the sequential stages of adulthood their level of civic involvement stays fairly constant, yet a decline is evident when one compares the involvement of different generations. Putnam states, "the decades that have seen a national deterioration in social capital are the very decades during which the numerical dominance of an exceptionally civic generation was replaced by the dominion of 'postcivic' cohorts."[117] Those born in the first four decades of the twentieth century are more civic-minded than the generations that have come after them.

Putnam points to two reasons why the level of civic engagement dropped in succeeding generations in the twentieth century. One major reason for the civic involvement of earlier generations is what he calls "the wartime Zeitgeist."[118] The two world wars in the first half of the century created a sense of solidarity among Americans, a solidarity that resulted in a high level of civic engagement. People from the more recent generations who have not experienced the bonding effects of war have felt less cohesion with other citizens,[119] and therefore they are less involved

---

113. Putnam, *Bowling Alone*, 223.

114. Ibid., 224.

115. Ibid., 236.

116. Ibid., 237.

117. Ibid., 255.

118. Ibid., 267.

119. Putnam is careful to point out that while war may have a cohesive effect, we must not use this to justify or glorify war (275–76). I suggest that while the war in Iraq seems to be producing this same type of solidarity in some parts of the US society, the

in activities that produce social capital. A second major reason is related to the television factor already addressed above. As Putnam points out, "the long civic generation was the last cohort of Americans to grow up without television. The more fully that any given generation was exposed to television in its formative years, the lower its civic engagement during adulthood."[120] The effects of television noted earlier have been less evident in the generations that reached adulthood before the 1960s because these generations were not significantly shaped by television during their child-hood years. To summarize, the drop in civic engagement is connected to changes between generations. More recent generations have not been bonded together by factors arising from war and they have been more shaped by the medium of television. For these two reasons they have been marked by a dramatic decline in social capital.

Putnam has pointed to several values that might underlie these changes. The workplace has come to be valued over family and com-munity. Individual spirituality has come to be valued over committed involvement in faith communities. People have come to value passive observation over active participation—whether in leisure activities, as-sociational membership, or political involvement. Before I consider how these values are related to the priesthood of all believers, I turn now to the work of a third cultural observer, Zygmunt Bauman.

Zygmunt Bauman on the Anxious Individual

Our society no longer provides communal vehicles of identity formation, argues Zygmunt Bauman. The individual is left with the responsibility and obligation to form his or her own identity, but the individual is not given the resources to do this.[121] As a result, ours is a society made up of anxious individuals.

---

effect nationally seems to be polarizing rather than bonding. While it may not produce cohesion, the Iraq war may in fact lead to a rise in civic involvement as people with differ-ent perspectives champion their causes. Would such involvement, born out of dissension rather than cohesion, lead to an increase in social capital? This will be fruitful subject for future research.

120. Putnam, *Bowling Alone*, 272.

121. Bauman, *The Individualized Society*, 5–6.

The choices for identity formation in our liquid culture are limited.[122] People can choose from an array of options to form their lives, but they are unaware of the conditions that limit their choices. Conditions are "things that happened to one, that came uninvited and would not leave if one wished them to go."[123] We take conditions for granted; they are seen as the givens of our situation. Within these conditions, the telling of life narratives forms identity. While people are not responsible for the conditions, they *are* responsible for the narratives they live and tell. Yet these narratives are restricted by the conditions that present the choices, and so our understandings of how we have lived and our expectations for how we can live are constrained by the conditions.[124]

Articulation is a concept that Bauman picks up to illuminate the process of identity formation. Articulations refer to the ways in which we relate practices to one another.[125] They allow us to incorporate our experiences into our life narratives. In our society, articulation has come to place all responsibility firmly on the shoulders of individuals: "all the messes into which one can get are assumed to be self-made and all the hot water into which one can fall is proclaimed to have been boiled by the hapless failures who have fallen into it."[126] Bauman continues:

> All articulations open up certain possibilities and close down some others. The distinctive feature of the stories told in our times is that they articulate individual lives in a way that excludes or suppresses (prevents from articulation) the possibility of tracking down the links connecting individual fate to the ways and means by which society as a whole operates; more to the point, it precludes the questioning of such ways and means by relegating them to the unexamined background of individual life pursuits and casting them as 'brute facts' which the story-teller can neither challenge nor negotiate, whether singly, severally, or collectively.[127]

122. Bauman uses the phrase "liquid modernity" because this culture is marked by fluidity of money, fluidity of relationships, and fluidity of location. See Bauman, *Liquid Modernity.*

123. Bauman, *The Individualized Society*, 6.

124. Ibid., 6–8.

125. Ibid., 8.

126. Ibid., 9.

127. Ibid.

Making articulations has become an individual task and the current articulations work against any changes in this. Our articulations keep us from questioning whether or not the set of conditions with which we are presented can in fact be changed.

Identity was once a given. People did not have to work to develop their identities. But as a result of individualization, the whole process of identity formation has now become a task rather than a given.[128] And whereas the primary question used to be one of means, now it is one of ends: what identity should a person try to pursue?[129] This is part of the dilemma of an individualized society.

An examination of democracy points to some of the consequences of individualization. Democracy always contains within it the struggle between freedom and security.[130] The struggle for much of democracy's history has been to assure freedom, but today the struggle is to assure security. Both aspects of society rely on the existence of citizens—that is, people who care about the common good. But individualization has turned the focus of people inward and has made them skeptical about the possibility or desirability of a common good.[131] People's focus is on pursuing what is good for themselves, thus the shift from discourse on a "just society" to discourse on "human rights."[132] In the past, the great fear was that the state would invade the private sphere. Bauman argues that the danger today is reversed. People are expecting society to consider first their own personal interests. Bauman speaks of this in terms of colonization. The fear was once that the public realm would colonize the private realm, but now "it is the private that colonizes the public space, squeezing out and chasing away everything which cannot be fully, without residue, translated into the vocabulary of private interests and pursuits."[133] Democracy requires the pursuit of the common good; individualization ignores the common good.

The individualization of identity formation and the exaltation of individuals' interests contribute to an anxious state of living. I will set forth

128. Ibid., 144.
129. Ibid., 147.
130. Ibid., 55.
131. Ibid., 49.
132. Ibid., 105.
133. Ibid., 107.

how Bauman works from several angles to show that anxiety arises from and contributes to the individualizing forces of our society.

The shifting nature of employment is one source of anxiety. The development of the market economy has led to a growing flexibility in the workplace. Companies at one time saw it as advantageous to employ people for the long-term. Today, in our "liquid" or "fluid" society, corporations are best served by quickly shifting their productive capacities to any place in the world that offers a slightly higher degree of profitability. Corporations are also rewarded for streamlining and downsizing.[134] These factors create an unstable employment situation. Because of these factors, people have now developed a short-term mentality. People no longer expect to work for one company for a long period of time. The fluid nature of employment results in a higher level of uncertainty and this uncertainty produces anxiety.

The precariousness of the employment arena is an individualizing force. Loyalties and commitments become obstacles to the fluidity required of the labor market.[135] The uncertainty associated with employment "divides instead of uniting, and since there is no telling who might wake up in what division, the idea of "common interests" grows ever more nebulous and in the end becomes incomprehensible. Fears, anxieties and grievances are made in such a way as to be suffered alone."[136] The uncertainty that arises from the unstable employment situation isolates people and severs mutual commitments and obligations.[137]

The relational dimension of uncertainty goes beyond the work place. It extends to family and neighbors as well. These once functioned as safety nets. Individuals who were thrown out of work or faced other hardships could retreat to the safety of family and neighbors to regroup. Today, however, these safety nets have huge holes in them. As a result, people have come to conceptualize interpersonal relationships in pragmatic terms, which "cannot generate lasting bonds, and most certainly not the bonds which are *presumed* to be lasting and *treated* as such. The bonds it does generate have inbuilt until-further-notice and withdrawal-at-will

134. Ibid., 26.

135. Ibid., 11–12.

136. Ibid., 24.

137. Ibid., 24, 156–57. Bauman points out that the poor are the only ones who do not experience uncertainty, but the dehumanizing and unjust nature of their certainty is seen by others as something to be feared more than uncertainty (116).

clauses and promise neither the granting nor the acquisition of rights and obligations."[138] The degeneration of social bonds leads to uncertainty and isolation, which result in anxiety.

Ambivalence is another force that contributes to anxiety. Bauman uses ambivalence to mean that "we cannot be sure what is going to happen, and so neither know how to behave, nor can predict what the outcome of our actions will be."[139] We have so many options before us that we are uncertain which ones to choose. The choice is complicated because it is unclear what the result of any given choice will be. Modernity sought to eliminate ambivalence, but the attempt has failed.[140] Bauman argues that ambivalence is not recognized as a societal problem. Rather, it is seen as a *personal* problem that each individual must solve on his or her own. To solve this problem, "we are bound to turn to the self-same market of commodified goods, services, and ideas (thus also, presumably, of counsels and therapies), which is the major production plant of ambivalence and its zealous and resourceful supplier."[141] It is a vicious circle.

In summary, Bauman argues that we are now a society of anxious individuals. One reason for this is that people are now responsible for creating their own identities, but they are not given the resources to do so; they are autonomous *de jure,* but not *de facto.* The private world is colonizing public spaces as individuals pursue their own best interests and seek to deal with their anxiety. This anxiety results from the instability of the work arena as well as from the collapse of other social networks such as family and neighbors. The rapidly shifting nature of our choices and the potential results of these choices result in ambivalence. Because of these factors, we live in an atmosphere of "ambient fear."[142]

Bauman, like Bellah, sees one of the basic values of individualism as the pursuit of one's own interests. A second value of individualism that becomes apparent from Bauman's analysis is that of individual identity formation. This institution shuns the idea that one's identity should be formed by or be contingent upon other relationships or structures. Each

138. Ibid., 86.
139. Ibid., 57.
140. Ibid., 65–67.
141. Ibid., 69.
142. Ibid., 83, 159. Bauman attributes this phrase to Marcus Doel and David Clarke.

individual is to construct his or her own identity in a way that is unencumbered by traditions or commitments.

Individualism and the Priesthood of All Believers

The institutions of individualism and the royal priesthood share the common value of celebrating each person's uniqueness. The correspondence of this value is only partial, however. Individualism celebrates this uniqueness for the benefit of the self. Within the royal priesthood this uniqueness is celebrated for both individual and corporate reasons. The fact that the Holy Spirit gifts people in diverse ways is affirmed in the priesthood of all believers. Within the context of this social structure people are encouraged to blossom into the fully unique people they are intended to be, but this uniqueness is given not just for the benefit of the individual; its primary purpose is for the building up of the body of Christ. The individuality that is part of the priesthood of all believers emerges from and serves the community. Its end is not an isolated individualized identity.

Bellah has described the primary value of utilitarian individualism as success. The institutional clash here emerges from the definition of success. Utilitarian individualism defines success in terms of financial advancement and a rise in one's social status. These terms do not characterize success as defined within the priesthood of all believers. Success within this priesthood is connected to the ways in which one cares for others, the extent to which one overcomes the distinctive status of the dominant culture, and the willingness of a person to be present with the other.

Expressive individualism has as its primary value positive feelings and personal satisfaction. People within the royal priesthood may certainly experience these feelings and satisfaction, but the pursuit of such feelings and personal satisfaction is not the determinative factor in life. On the one hand, those in the royal priesthood are invited to engage the full range of emotions. This includes not only the exalted feelings of resurrection celebration but also the suffering oppression and darkness of the crucifixion. On the other hand, Christians are to be guided by more than just feelings. Christians are called to make choices that are congruous with the rules, paradigms, and narratives of God. Often these patterns of living make no sense to the person whose primary value is attaining positive emotional feelings.

Individualism has a positive bearing on the priesthood of all believers to the extent that it fosters individual responsibility. Though the royal priesthood is a corporate entity, this fact does not take away responsibility from the individuals within it. While the community is accountable for living out its divinely given nature, this in no way means that individuals within the community have the option of passive membership. Each individual is accountable for his or her commitments and actions within and on behalf of the community. The institution of individualism helps to highlight this responsibility and accountability.

A clash between individualism and the priesthood of all believers is evident in each institution's view of identity formation. Bauman has pointed out how postmodern culture calls for individuals to form their own identities in ways unencumbered by traditions and obligations and Putnam has shown that postmodern culture promotes an individual form of spirituality. In contrast, within the priesthood of all believers, an individual's identity and spiritual formation are rooted in a communal structure grounded in God's narrative. A person's identity *is* connected to a tradition. A person's identity *is* formed in relation to others. Christian identity formation in fact assumes a communal context. The priesthood is a communal institution—we are not just isolated individual priests. We are priests in the royal priesthood; we are people grounded in a social structure.

I argued in ch. 3 that a trinitarian ecclesiology calls for a common priesthood in which all believers participate. Each Christian is called to active involvement in the mission of God. Putnam has shown how the institution of individualism fosters passive observation rather than active participation. The passive nature of individualism is at odds with the participatory nature of the royal priesthood.

Finally, the ongoing process of being formed as priests requires a belief that the royal priesthood matters in the long term. But Bauman argues that the precariousness that marks our lives today has shaped us to believe that *nothing* matters in the long term.[143] It is only the immediate that matters. If this is the case, then an institution that asks for life-long attention and which may only reveal its benefits in the long run makes no sense. However, for those who have been formed by the institutional values of the priesthood of all believers, meanings and relationships cannot

143. Ibid., 154–55.

be understood only in the immediate moment. Our forming narratives are historical in character—they took place over a long period of time and they reflect a God who shapes and leads his people generation after generation. A long-term perspective characterizes the priesthood of all believers.

TECHNIQUE

Technique, a term used by Jacques Ellul,[144] is a third institution that dominates our culture today. To understand Ellul's conception of the technological system, we must distinguish between the French words *techniques, technologie,* and *technique.*[145] Ellul uses the word *techniques* to refer to concrete realities such as genetics, modes of production, or environmentalism. *Techniques* are methods or patterns for carrying out actions. This is somewhat equivalent to how "technologies" is used in English, although in English the term is most often given a narrower meaning that focuses on things such as electronics and other complex products. *Technologie,* as used by Ellul, is the science that studies *techniques.* Ellul is not primarily concerned with either *techniques* nor *technologie.* Ellul's primary concern is with *technique.* He uses this term to refer broadly to an ensemble of practices.[146] *Technique* is much bigger than machines or electronics or a particular way of producing something. When Ellul speaks of *technique* he is referring to ways in which processes function in society. *Technique* has been present in all civilizations. For example, primitive cultures had the *technique* of hunting, and later cultures had the *technique* of metal-

---

144. Ellul first addressed the technological phenomenon in his 1954 work, *The Technological Society* (ET 1964). He continued to address this concept with his 1977 work, *The Technological System* (ET 1980) and his 1988 work, *The Technological Bluff* (ET 1990). The fact that this framework, which Ellul first set forth 50 years ago, is still fresh and helpful today attests to the conceptual soundness of Ellul's work.

145. Ellul's most focused discussion of these terms can be found in Ellul, *The Technological System,* 23–27, 32–33. Also helpful is his discussion of *technique* found in Ellul, *The Technological Society,* xxv–xxvi, 3–22. and the translator's notes in Ellul, *The Technological Bluff,* ix.

146. See translator's note in Ellul, *The Technological Society,* x. *Technique* and the English "technique" have an identical spelling, but they do not mean the same thing. In spite of this, translators of Ellul have often used the latter to translate the former. Where I use this word, I have chosen to leave it untranslated and thus italicized in order to emphasize its particular meaning here.

lurgy.[147] Ellul's interest is in understanding the role that *technique* plays in Western culture today.[148] As do Ellul and his translators, I will use "technological system," "technological phenomenon," and "technology" as synonyms for *technique*.

I will now discuss how Ellul's concept functions as an institution. Then I will describe George Ritzer's current work on McDonaldization, which can be understood in terms of *technique*. Both writers give us insight into how this powerful institution is at work in our culture. I will conclude by describing the relationship between *technique* and the priesthood of all believers.

Jacques Ellul's Technique *as Institution*

Technique is both an environment and a system. It refers to patterns of organization and relationship. It is the ensemble of practices that define our existence. *Technique* describes the ways in which resources are used. In Western society today, this technological system has become the determining factor; it shapes every aspect of our lives.[149]

Technique has become a mediation between humans and everything else.[150] Humans have come to experience life only through the mediation of technological activity. We think of humans as the mediating factor in society, but in fact they are already within the technological system. The system itself is a mediation or environment, and "ultimately, the technological environment . . . presumes to replace all of the natural environment, performing all of its functions."[151]

As a mediation it has three characteristics. First, it is an autonomous mediation. It does not depend upon us or anything else for its continuing existence. This autonomous mediation is exclusive—other mediations are

147. Ibid., 23.

148. In reading Ellul's works, which do not have the same translator, the reader will avoid confusion by noting that *technique* is translated as "technique" in *The Technological Society* but is translated as "technology" in *The Technological System*. In *The Technological Bluff*, the word is once again translated as "technique."

149. Ellul, *The Technological System*, 18.

150. Ibid., 35.

151. Ibid., 46.

pushed out.[152] Second, the mediation of technique is sterilizing.[153] It does not draw on the past nor project into the future and it seeks to reduce the messy or disorderly to a single voice which will relate the individual to the world in ways that do not disturb the system. Third, while it mediates every other relationship of humanity, technology's relationship with humanity is *not* mediated: "the social or individual consciousness today is formed directly by the presence of technology, by man's immersion in that environment, without the mediation of thought, for which technology would only be an object, without the mediation of culture."[154] Whereas once thought or culture mediated between humanity and the technological system, now the technological system mediates between humanity and thought or culture. A direct relationship exists only between humans and *technique* itself.

By nature, *technique* is self-perpetuating. When problems arise, the technological system allows no room for other mediations to provide solutions; the only possible solutions are those that arise from within the system. As Ellul puts it:

> The more the technological universe expresses itself in intense and continuous noise, the greater the need for silence, the more research and money must be applied to creating silence. The same holds true for the pollution of air or water. But here we are faced with problems that have to be solved not only by new productions, but also by services and organizations [which are also technologies].[155]

To put it another way, new technologies must be developed to overcome the shortcomings of technology; technology is seen as the only source available for overcoming these shortcomings.

To get at other dimensions of *technique* we can conceptualize it as a system. Like all systems, the whole is greater than the sum of its parts.[156] The system cannot be understood simply by studying the individual technologies that are part of it. Therefore Ellul finds it useless to focus

---

152. Ibid., 36–37. This issue of autonomy will be addressed more fully below in talking about *technique* as a system.

153. Ibid., 37.

154. Ibid., 38.

155. Ibid., 63.

156. Ibid., 89.

on any one part of the system such as cars or computers. He claims that these specific technologies make no sense except within the context of the technological system.[157] As an open system, technology by its very nature demands progress and change.[158] This system is flexible, a feature that lets it overcome and absorb tensions that arise within it.[159]

Ellul sets forth four primary characteristics of the technological phenomenon. First, as already noted above, *technique* is autonomous. By this, Ellul means that "technology ultimately depends only on itself, it maps its own route, it is a prime and not a secondary factor, it must be regarded as an 'organism' tending toward closure and self-determination: it is an end in itself."[160] The technological system has taken on a life of its own and whereas it may have once served ends determined by people, it now defines and serves its own ends. Technology is autonomous from the state, from politics, and from culture. It is an illusion that any of these can control technology. Technology is often tied closely to economics, but Ellul argues that, although a relationship certainly exists between the two, the technological system *dominates* economics; it must not to be equated with economics.[161]

A second characteristic of *technique* is unity. The system is made up of numerous subsystems that are interdependent. These subsystems take diverse forms, but they are all "obedient to a common regularity,"[162] they all conform to the nature of the technological system. For example, transportation is related to urbanization, industrial production, and mass consumption.[163] These areas are interdependent and spawn new technologies that are related to them. The system even spawns technologies which organize and regulate this unicity.[164] One consequence of this complete interdependence is that it is impossible to distinguish between

---

157. Ibid., 107. The continuing relevance of Ellul's work is due to this fact that he focuses on the technological system, not on individual technologies. Technologies have changed immensely in the last five decades, but because he focuses on *technique* and not techniques, Ellul's analysis remains relevant today.

158. Ibid., 78–80, 116.

159. Ibid., 110.

160. Ibid., 125.

161. Ibid., 138.

162. Ibid., 156.

163. Ibid., 159.

164. Ibid., 163.

good technologies and bad technologies.[165] A technology developed for a particular use cannot be confined to that use and therefore its goodness or badness is shifting and uncontrollable. Ellul points out that this unity results in fragility. When any part of the system hits a snag, the whole system is subject to upheaval. This was seen in the 2003 power outage in the eastern United States where millions of people were affected by the failure of a link in the power grid hundreds of miles away in Ohio. Another consequence of this unity is that problems cannot be addressed individually, but must be considered in light of the greater system.

A third characteristic of the technological system is universality. This universality has two aspects. First, technology reaches into every nook and cranny around the globe. There is a geographical universality to *technique*. Second, technology permeates every area of our daily lives. It touches our work, our family relations, and our free time. Every human activity has come to be technologically oriented:

> There is a technology of reading (speed reading), as well as a technology of chewing. Every single sport is becoming more and more technological. There is a technology for cultural animation and for chairing a meeting. And this list could be stretched out ad infinitum.[166]

We can no longer find any aspect of life that is not impacted by *technique*. Even religion is subject to technicization.[167] People are looking for a procedure for religious experience and they seek to identify results as a means of comparing religious technologies.

Ellul's fourth characteristic of *technique* is totalization. On one hand, technology is specializing.[168] More and more specific technologies are constantly being developed. The flip side of this specialization is totalization.[169] As technologies become more specialized, they move towards total extension in our lives. The technological system works to integrate every aspect of life into a new totality.[170]

165. Ibid., 164.
166. Ibid., 170.
167. Ibid., 174–75.
168. Ibid., 199.
169. Ibid., 199–204.
170. Ibid., 203.

How does *technique* qualify as an institution? The technological system certainly provides normative patterns which is a characteristic of an institution. Its patterns are both explicit and implicit. Bellah described institutions as mediating our shared lives. Ellul has argued that *technique* has come to mediate every aspect of our lives. Bellah pointed out that institutions carry within them values. The technological phenomenon has been viewed as value-neutral, it has been viewed as a system that can be utilized by a variety of value systems, but Ellul has argued that this neutrality is an illusion.[171]

What, then, are the values embedded in *technique*? One value is that of progress. Progress is part of the ideology of the system. The system tells us that progress is a fundamental good and the system demands progress to sustain its existence.[172] Those who would question the good of progress are pushed to the side by the powerful flow of the system.

The technological system *de*values individuality. On the surface, it appears that the choices of individuals are expanded because they now have many more options to choose from. However, these options all conform to the nature of the system and therefore they serve the continued hegemony of the system. The uniqueness of individuals is allowed only within certain parameters.

The most powerful driving value of *technique* is efficiency. Just as water always follows the path of least resistance down a hill, so *technique* always seeks the most efficient way of doing things. The drive for greater efficiency lies behind the development of *technique*.[173] Efficiency can be described as the *telos* of the technological system. Here again we see what was described above as the sanitizing character of *technique*. Tradition and aesthetics are caste aside except where they occasionally serve the goal of efficiency. Technology can advance in the most efficient way only when unencumbered by obligations to any institution outside itself. When Ellul states that "total technization occurs when every aspect of human life is subjected to control and manipulation, to experimentation and observation, so that a demonstrable efficiency is achieved everywhere,"[174] he is pointing to the fundamental and teleological role of efficiency in the

171. Ibid., 154–55.
172. Ibid., 80.
173. Ellul, *The Technological Society*, 20.
174. Ellul, *The Technological System*, 82.

technological phenomenon. Values such as fidelity, mutual obligation, or non-coercion have no independent place to stand in the institution of *technique*. They can exist only to the extent that they serve efficiency.

The system would have us believe otherwise, however, and this is what Ellul labels "the technological bluff." *Technique* would have us believe that it in fact works for positive values and does not have negative side affects. *Technique* would have us believe that it alone can provide the solutions to the problems our world faces. Ellul describes the bluff in this way:

> The bluff consists essentially of rearranging everything in terms of technical progress, which with prodigious diversification offers us in every direction such varied possibilities that we can imagine nothing else . . . . And when I say bluff, it is because so many successes and exploits are ascribed to techniques (without regard for the cost or utility or risk), because technique is regarded in advance as the only solution to collective problems (unemployment, Third World misery, pollution, war) or individual problems (health, family life, even the meaning of life), and because at the same time it is seen as the only chance for progress and development in society. There is bluff here because the effective possibilities are multiplied a hundredfold in such discussions and the negative aspects are radically concealed.[175]

This institution contains a powerful set of values, but the institution will not admit to this. Such an admission would open *technique* up to evaluation. While particular technologies can be set forth for evaluation, the system as a whole assumes that it is above this, that it is a given and not something that can be considered morally.

In summary, *technique* is an institution that seeks to mediate between humans and everything else. It is a system that is greater than the sum of its parts—it cannot be understood by studying technologies. It is autonomous, unifying, universal, and totalizing. Hidden within this institution is a powerful set of values that include progress and efficiency. The institution seeks to absorb or annihilate any other institutions that would dare to challenge its methods, roles, or outcomes.

I turn now to the work of George Ritzer, whose work on McDonaldization gives further credence to Ellul's claims regarding *technique*.

---

175. Ellul, *The Technological Bluff*, xvi.

George Ritzer on Our McDonaldized Society

In his social criticism, George Ritzer uses the fast-food chain McDonald's as both an example and a metaphor of what is happening in American society.[176] He coins the word "McDonaldization" and defines it as "the process by which the principles of the fast-food restaurant are coming to dominate more and more sectors of American society as well as the rest of the world."[177] He describes how McDonald's operates and shows how these principles of operation extend far beyond American culture.

McDonald's has become a global icon. It has moved from the corners of our streets into our educational campuses and office buildings. It has moved from America to nations around the world. Ritzer contends that McDonald's is not just a fast-food business that sells hamburgers, but has become a cultural symbol, even a sacred institution.[178] Though Ritzer gives many specific details regarding the way in which McDonald's functions, the fast-food chain is representative of a much larger phenomenon. He sets forth four dimensions to this institution: efficiency, calculability, predictability, and control through non-human means.

Efficiency is the most important aspect of McDonaldization. It is the controlling process from which the other three dimensions proceed. This is an on-going process that builds on itself. Although optimal efficiency is seldom attained due to the intervention of less controllable factors, successive approximations move toward this end. The process of food preparation at McDonald's is a model of efficiency. Partially sliced buns were replaced with fully sliced buns because this was determined to be more efficient. Paper waxed in a particular way is used between hamburger patties to allow the patties to slide onto the grill in the most efficient way.[179]

Efficiency leads to speed. As a result of efficiency, every aspect of our lives is moving more and more rapidly.[180] The streamlined process of food production at McDonald's allows us to eat more rapidly. The educational system is being streamlined with things like computer-scored multiple choice tests that allow for quicker grading. In addition to streamlin-

176. George Ritzer, *The McDonaldization of Society.*

177. Ibid., 1.

178. Ibid., 7.

179. Ibid., 42.

180. Ibid., 40.

ing the process, simplifying the product makes for greater efficiency.[181] McDonald's uses simple recipes and has a limited menu. This simplifying tendency is exhibited in specialization. Jiffy Lube has specialized in oil changes, and by keeping their service options simple, they are able to focus on ways to carry out these services in the most efficient way. A third way that McDonaldization pursues efficiency is by putting the customer to work.[182] Examples of this are having diners bus their own tables and having shoppers scan their own items in the checkout line. Streamlining, simplifying the product, and putting the customer to work all speed up the process, which leads to greater efficiency. Ritzer acknowledges that greater efficiency has its benefits—he sees it as advantageous when consumers can obtain what they want more quickly and with less effort.[183] However, his main focus is on the ways in which efficiency is dehumanizing.[184]

Ellul argued that the technological system pushes out processes that are not themselves technical. This is manifest in Ritzer's second dimension of McDonaldization: calculability. In order to attain the greatest level of efficiency, processes must be quantifiable. We must be able to measure a process in some way in order to know if we are becoming more efficient at carrying out the process. Non-quantifiable processes are pushed out of the system.

Calculability emphasizes quantity over quality.[185] The educational system emphasizes test scores, quantity of publications, and the ranking of institutions. The health care system emphasizes the number of patients a doctor sees in a day. While calculability may allow for a greater number of products and services, Ritzer argues that this emphasis on quantity results in mediocre products and services.

Predictability is a third dimension of McDonaldization. Efficiency is enhanced by the predictability of behavior, products, and processes. Ritzer states, "to achieve predictability, a rationalized society emphasizes discipline, order, systematization, formalization, routine, consistency, and

181. Ibid., 55–57.
182. Ibid., 57–61.
183. Ibid., 40.
184. Ibid., 40–41, 61.
185. Ibid., 64–82.

methodical operation."[186] Many of the interactions that employees have with customers are now scripted. Fast food and retail employees are told how to greet customers. Telemarketers and theme park employees follow scripts. Scripting brings a higher level of predictability to the process which allows the system to function more smoothly, although the human factor keeps the process from being completely predictable and therefore glitches in the system are inevitable.

Predictability is not just demanded by efficiency; it is demanded by consumers as well. Ritzer argues that we have been socialized to desire predictability rather than uncertainty. We like the predictability of going into a McDonald's, whether it is in Los Angeles or New York or Moscow or Hong Kong. We like knowing exactly what we will get when we check into a Super 8 Motel. We like predictability because it minimizes danger and unpleasantness.[187] Ritzer states that predictability can be reassuring and he sees the safety it can provide as a benefit. His critique of predictability is not as pointed as his critiques of other aspects of McDonaldization. In his view, the main problem with predictability is that it creates a boring world.[188]

The fourth dimension of McDonaldization that Ritzer sets forth is control through non-human technology. Here he is thinking about technology broadly: he is not just thinking about electronics and machines, but also about regulations, procedures, and knowledge (although he is not quite thinking about technology as a whole system, as does Ellul). Ritzer makes a distinction between human and non-human technology: "a *human technology* (a screwdriver, for example) is controlled by people; a *non-human technology* (the order window at the drive-through, for instance) controls people."[189] By using non-human technology, McDonaldization creates a more predictable, more controllable system.

Many processes that were once carried out by humans are now carried out by nonhuman technologies. Fast food restaurants use lettuce and cheese that is pre-shredded by machines because this allows for more control of the process. McDonald's and others use automatic French fry machines so that human judgment can be eliminated from the process,

---

186. Ibid., 83.
187. Ibid., 100.
188. Ibid., 103.
189. Ibid., 104.

and thus a higher level of control can be obtained. In the field of medicine, the managed care system has taken away from doctors much of the ability to decide how long an individual can stay in the hospital. Not just employees, but customers as well are subject to such control. "Conveyer systems" work to move customers through theme parks and retail stores in ways that allow for the greatest efficiency.[190] Ritzer again points out benefits but focuses on the negative aspects of this technological control. In the end, laments Ritzer, "more and more people will lose the opportunity, and perhaps the ability, to think for themselves."[191]

With the language of Weber, Ritzer's fundamental critique of McDonaldization is its irrationality of rationality.[192] Rational systems eventually spawn irrationalities. Bureaucracies that were constructed to increase efficiency become ponderous behemoths. Services and products that were to serve humans end up dehumanizing us. We are not free to simply opt out of the system, because rationality has become what Weber referred to as the "iron cage."[193] People are trapped in the iron cage of rationality, which subjects them to the irrationalities of the system. Ritzer believes these irrationalities have become far greater than the benefits of the system.[194]

In summary, Ritzer notes four values that are embedded in McDonaldization: efficiency, calculability, predictability, and control through nonhuman means. This technological system that once served us has now come to control us. This is the irrationality of the rational system.

Technique *and the Priesthood of All Believers*

The work of both Ellul and Ritzer points to efficiency as the primary value of the institution of *technique*. All processes, activities, and relationships have come to be scrutinized in terms of their efficiency. This institutional value patterns our work, our recreation, and our relationships.

190. Ibid., 113.
191. Ibid., 122.
192. Ibid., 24–25, 123–45.
193. Ibid., 25.
194. Ibid., 145.

How does the value of efficiency relate to the priesthood of all believers? As Ritzer has pointed out, people are much less predictable than machines. The ways we act are connected to a whole range of inputs including our emotions, traditions, and family influences. We may often seek to make rational choices, but such choices are never free from these other non-rational influences and therefore we are not predictable. Even when the rational choice is obvious, we do not always choose it. Predictability is required for efficiency to be maximized and so *technique* sees humans, because they are unpredictable, as a negative factor in the system. As Ellul has indicated, the technological system devalues people. This is a stark contrast to the royal priesthood in which human beings are a *prime* value. Each person is to be viewed as a unique and highly prized creation of God; trinitarian differentiation is mirrored in the royal priesthood. The priesthood of all believers understands that each and every person has a valuable role to play in God's mission in this world. The values of the institution of *technique* clash here with the values of the institution of the royal priesthood. When efficiency is made the ultimate value, it works against this value of the priesthood of all believers.

Efficiency shapes what we look for in religion. The on-going pursuit of efficiency has taught us to value greater speed and less effort and so we look for religious forms and experiences that promise speed and ease. But greater speed and less effort are antithetical to the process required for the formation of the royal priesthood. With more than a hint of sarcasm, Ellul asks, "why bother with the long asceticism of spiritual exercises, like Ignatius de Loyola, if a pill can give us the same result?"[195] The problem here is that Christian formation does not take place in accordance with the demands of efficiency.

Built into the institution of *technique* is the process of evaluation. Evaluation is required for systems to move towards efficiency. This impulse for evaluation has positive potential for the priesthood of all believers. The royal priesthood is passed down from generation to generation. Whenever the passing on of customs, practices, or structures occurs, the thoughts and reasons behind them can become obscured. The process of evaluation is a positive force when it encourages us to justify and claim anew our understanding and embodiment of the royal priesthood.

195. Ellul, *The Technological System*, 174–75.

Is progress good? As Christians we are rooted in a tradition. Our tradition is historical, that is, it has existed and been shaped over the course of time. The tradition includes elements that change as well as elements that do not change. The technological society seems to value progress and change uncritically. The Christian tradition incorporates into itself some forms of progress and change, but rejects others. *Technique* assumes that all progress is good. Aspects of the Christian tradition are marked by a constancy that the technological system seeks to caste aside for the sake of progress.

Ellul's analysis has shown the hegemonic nature of *technique*. The royal priesthood rejects the notion that individuals are to serve *technique*. Christians are to have institutional loyalties and are to be formed by institutional influences, but these are not loyalties to or influences of *technique*. It is the priesthood of all believers, the body of Christ, that is to have this institutional role. And the nature of this institution is not hegemonic. The institution does not seek to force itself on people. In correspondence to the trinitarian relationships, it is non-dominating.

Ellul has argued that *technique* has transformed the structure of society from hierarchical to egalitarian. He states, "all inequality, all discrimination (e.g., racial), all particularism, are condemned by technology."[196] The priesthood of all believers, too, is marked by egalitarianism. Do we have a coincidence of values here? Yes . . . in part. The technological system rejects inequality and discrimination and thus can be a supporting factor in fostering a priesthood of equals, a priesthood that also rejects inequality and discrimination. But the egalitarianism of *technique* may be more related to the indiscriminate embedding of all people in the institution rather than an egalitarian treatment of people once they are in the system. Also, that the egalitarianism of *technique* condemns particularism is problematic. The differentiation of charisms points to a *celebration* of particularism. The driving force for egalitarianism differs drastically between the two institutions. For *technique*, the driving force is the reduction of all things to "commensurable and rational factors."[197] For the priesthood of all believers, the driving force is the validation of human dignity and worth that God has assigned to every human being.

---

196. Ibid., 71.
197. Ibid.

Technique is a commanding force. As with globalization and individualism, at points *technique's* values coincide with the values of the royal priesthood. However, the primary thrust of *technique* undercuts the values that characterize the priesthood of all believers. For Christians, who live in the technological society and in the royal priesthood at the same time, value conflicts will arise and choices must be made regarding institutional loyalties.

SUMMARY

I have related the priesthood of all believers to postmodern culture because the priesthood of all believers exists as an alternative community within, not outside of, the dominant culture. Members of this alternative community must understand the dominant culture around them because the priesthood of all believers is always pushed and pulled by the cultural context within which it is located. Without an understanding of the host culture, the values of that culture will seep into and warp the nature of the royal priesthood.

Using the framework of institutions has provided us with a way of understanding several dominant forces within postmodernity that seek to pattern our actions and relationships. Globalization, individualism, and *technique* all contain within them value sets that would shape us. These values, as we have seen, clash at many points with the values embedded in the royal priesthood. A keen awareness of the tension between the institution of the priesthood of all believers and the institutions of postmodernity will help the church to be true to its nature.

The analysis I have undertaken in this chapter shows some of the challenges of living out the ecclesiology set forth in chapter three. This analysis of the relation between postmodern institutions and the priesthood of all believers aims at a constructive purpose. Bellah has noted that "institutions are very much dependent on language: what we cannot imagine and express in language has little chance of becoming a sociological reality."[198] I have attempted here to imagine the royal priesthood engaged with its host culture and yet holding steadfastly to its own values. My hope is that this will contribute to the ongoing existence of the priesthood of all believers as a sociological reality.

198. Bellah, *The Good Society*, 15.

FIVE

Congregational Practices and the Priesthood of All Believers

"Mind the gap!" This is the recorded message one hears when stepping from the platform onto the tube in London. It is an apt challenge for anyone doing theology and reflecting on congregations. Often there is a gap between our *stated* theology and our *lived* theology. We struggle to hold together our beliefs and our practices. Amy Plantinga Pauw points out that this was the case for Jonah. Jonah had true beliefs (and got good results!), but although he believed that God was a gracious and merciful God who was willing to relent from punishing (Jonah 4:2), the way Jonah carried out his role as prophet was incongruous with his beliefs.[1] The same gap often emerges in our local congregations today. We claim certain faith commitments, but then we often live in ways that are inconsistent with these claims. At these points, our beliefs, our practices, or both need to be modified.

In this chapter I will attempt to "mind the gap" between a theology of the priesthood of all believers and the on-going life of the local church. The priesthood of all believers can be re-embodied and re-conceptualized by reflecting on and engaging in the Christian practices resident within congregations. By engaging in Christian practices, limp and pallid congregations can be reinvigorated to live as the royal priesthood.

While *all* practices and actions have theological content (implicit or explicit), good *Christian* practices—for which I am advocating—are explicitly grounded theologically and are subject to evaluation based on

---

1. Pauw, "Attending to the Gaps between Beliefs and Practices," 37–40.

these theological claims. While practices are shaped by our theology, the inverse is also true and valid: our theology is shaped by our practices. The understanding of practices in this chapter, therefore, views beliefs and actions in a mutually informing relationship.

In the first section, we will explore an understanding of practices that builds on the work of Alasdair MacIntyre and considers what must be added to his conception in order to speak of *Christian* practices. In the second section, we will consider five Christian practices—witness, the Lord's supper, discernment, friendship, and confession—and then sketch their contours in MacIntyrian terms, survey some of the meanings embedded in these practices, and make connections between these practices and the priesthood of all believers. In the final section, I will suggest that these practices are best nurtured by congregational leaders who focus on interpretation and meaning-making. As congregations engage in Christian practices, we are 1) reshaped to better reflect our stated theology of the priesthood of all believers in our lives (corporately and individually), and 2) our understandings of the priesthood of all believers are re-imagined.

I intend for my ideas in this chapter to have a propositional rather than imperative tone to them. These are not the only ways a congregation can live as the priesthood of all believers. I have in mind a contextual theology for the church in the United States. I hold that these ideas are relevant for the whole range of church structures, from the hierarchical structure of the Catholic Church to the looser structures in the Free Church tradition, although different approaches may be required within different traditions and cultures. I assume that Christians in other contexts will find enriching ways to critique these ideas and will add, delete, and modify these ideas in order to best address their contexts. At the same time, while the forms may vary, I hold that the heart of the matter here is relevant to the church universal. God has called *all* Christians to be part of God's royal priesthood, a priesthood that transcends cultural differences, economic levels, racial groupings, and all other potentially stratifying categorizations. This universal priesthood is an important channel through which God has chosen to carry forth God's mission to the world.

THE NATURE OF SOCIAL PRACTICES

She is a practicing Catholic. He'll be home after baseball practice. After medical school she wants to start a private practice. The word "practice" has a broad range of meanings in popular usage. In addition to popular usages, practice has come to be used across a wide swath of academia as a way of understanding social life, and the technical meanings given this idea are as varied as in popular usage. As philosopher and social theorist Theodore Schatzki notes, practices have become an important concept in a range of disciplines including philosophy, cultural theory, history, sociology, anthropology, science, and technological studies.[2] The various uses have some general features in common—minimally, practices are conceived as arrays of activities—but no unified understanding or theory of practices exists.[3]

In the previous chapter I explored three institutions of postmodernity. In this chapter, we will want to consider what is the relationship between institutions and practices. Institutions can be described as bundles of practices. An institution provides the structure or parameters within which a practice is carried out. Jeffrey Stout asserts, "without some sort of sustaining institutions, the practice would change dramatically for the worse, if not collapse altogether."[4] Similarly, Alasdair MacIntyre asserts, "no practices can survive for any length of time unsustained by institutions."[5] Practices shape institutions and institutions shape practices. So the priesthood of all believers—an institution—is a necessary container within which a set of practices cohere, and the way in which these practices are carried out shapes the priesthood of all believers.

Both MacIntyre and Stout point out that the relationship between institutions and practices is intimate but troubled.[6] While institutions are essential for the survival of practices, institutions can also siphon off the energy of a practice and institutions can besmirch the integrity of a practice.[7] My intent in this project is to capitalize on the *positive* potential in this relationship. The priesthood of all believers can be re-conceptual-

---

2. Schatzki, "Introduction: Practice Theory," 1.

3. Ibid., 2. In this introductory chapter Schatzki provides a helpful overview of the various practice theories. Also helpful is Barnes's discussion of practices in the same volume. See Barnes, "Practice as Collective Action."

4. Stout, *Ethics after Babel*, 274.

5. MacIntyre, *After Virtue*, 194.

6. See ibid. and Stout, *Ethics after Babel*, 274.

7. MacIntyre is interested in how the exercise of virtues contributes to the integrity of practices. For his discussion of practices and institutions in relation to the virtues, see MacIntyre, *After Virtue*, 195–96.

ized and re-embodied in congregations by attending to congregational practices.

Alasdair MacIntyre's Conception of Social Practices

My discussion will build on the specific conception of practices set forth by Alasdair MacIntyre and extended by others. MacIntyre, in seeking to identify a common background for varied understandings of virtues, identifies practices as providing the necessary context. He provides a definition of practices that includes several key components. By a practice MacIntyre means,

> any coherent and complex form of socially established coopera- tive human activity through which goods internal to that form of activity are realized in the course of trying to achieve those stan- dards of excellence which are appropriate to, and partially defini- tive of, that form of activity, with the result that human powers to achieve excellence, and human conceptions of the ends and goods involved, are systematically extended.[8]

The first thing we must note about practices thus defined is that they are socially established. To be a practice means that an activity has a history. Craig Dykstra elaborates on MacIntyre's idea of social establishment: "practice is participation in a cooperatively formed pattern of activity that emerges out of a complex tradition of interactions among many people sustained over a long period of time."[9] This means that we cannot invent an activity today and have it count as a practice because it will not contain within it a history, a tradition. Time is required for a practice to become socially established.

The fact that practices are socially established—that is, that they are grounded in tradition—does not mean that they are static. Practices evolve and are reshaped by the practitioners. And yet, although a practice may not currently be carried out in the exact way as was done historically, it is still shaped by that history and thus carries that history within itself. Fly fishing can serve as an example here. This is an activity that is steeped in traditions, but the graphite rods and the high-tech fly lines used today are significantly different than the rods and lines used in this practice

8. Ibid., 187.

9. Dykstra, "Reconceiving Practice in Theological Inquiry and Education," 170.

decades ago. Casting techniques have been handed on from generation to generation, but today, through books and videos, a budding young fly fisherman can explore approaches that go beyond those that his father or grandfather taught him. Fly-fishing is grounded in history, but it is not frozen in history.

We must not allow this possibility for adaptation to obscure the basic characteristic of practices as grounded in a tradition. As Dykstra notes, an action that is *not* grounded in a tradition is a group activity, not a practice.[10] If an action lacks a history, it is not—at least, not *yet*—a practice.

This historical dimension ties into the next part of MacIntyre's definition: a practice is also a cooperative human activity.[11] Practices are inherently communal. They are carried out by groups of people, and because of this, practices shape both individual and communal identity. Only communal activities can be extended over generations—an activity carried out solely by an individual will die with that individual. An activity must be carried out by whole communities of people if it is to have a history, a tradition. As a socially established activity, a practice is also by definition a cooperative human activity.

An individual can do something by him- or herself and still be participating in a practice. How can this be? Doesn't this contradict what was just said about a practice being a cooperative activity? Not necessarily. A person carrying out an activity alone can be doing so within the stream of a tradition and in a way that is connected to other practitioners, even if these practitioners are not physically present. Dykstra offers the example of prayer. He points out that prayer "is cooperative because we pray, even when praying alone, as participants in the praying of the church."[12] In the same way, my example of fly-fishing can be understood as cooperative. Even if I go fly-fishing alone, I am guided by a set of fishing regulations, conventions of courtesy regarding how closely I can fish to others I might encounter on the same stream, and a fly-fishing code that expects me to release most of the fish I catch so that future fishers will also have fish to

---

10. Ibid., 171.

11. In the context of our discussion, "human" can be assumed, but this assumption cannot be made in the broader range of literature on practices because, as Schatzki notes, "a significant 'posthumanist' minority centered in science and technology studies avers . . . that the activities bound into practices also include those of nonhumans such as machines and the objects of scientific investigation" ("Introduction: Practice Theory," 2).

12. Dykstra, "Reconceiving Practice in Theological Inquiry and Education," 170.

catch. In MacIntyre's conception, cooperative activities include activities done by individuals alone when these activities are grounded in a tradition and are part of a larger cooperative effort.

Let me pause to give an example of something that is *not* a practice: getting the newspaper in the morning. A person may go through the same routine each morning: preparing a cup of coffee, putting on slippers, walking down the driveway with coffee in hand, picking up the newspaper, and returning to the front porch to read it. This may be a firmly established routine, but it is not a practice. There is nothing complex about this activity, it is not grounded in a tradition, and it would be a stretch to construe this as a cooperative human activity. Furthermore, getting the newspaper in the morning does not qualify as a practice because it does not have goods internal to it.

What are internal goods? These are goods or rewards that can only be had by participating in the practice. MacIntyre uses the example of a child playing chess.[13] Imagine that a child is offered candy for playing and winning a game of chess. The candy is a good external to playing chess. There are ways other than by playing and winning a game of chess to acquire candy. Hopefully the child will come to love the game of chess because of the analytical skills involved and the satisfaction of carrying out a creative strategy. These reasons for playing are *internal* goods. Only playing chess or some other similar game can have these goods.[14] Another way to put this is that the goal of a practice is found—at least in part—within the practice itself.

Two more points expand our understanding of internal goods. First, MacIntyre holds that only those who are engaged in the practice can adequately identify and evaluate the goods internal to it. MacIntyre asserts, "those who lack the relevant experience are incompetent thereby as judges of internal goods."[15] I turn to my fly-fishing example for illustration. I have a friend who repeatedly expresses her bewilderment at the fact that I catch fish and then *let them go!* I have tried to explain to her why this is such an enjoyable activity for me, but she remains bewildered. This illustrates MacIntyre's point that the goods internal to a practice are

13. MacIntyre, *After Virtue*, 188.

14. Jeffrey Stout, a sometime critic of MacIntyre, has great appreciation for MacIntyre's conception of practices. This idea of internal goods is the most important aspect of practices in Stout's view. See Stout, *Ethics after Babel*, 267.

15. MacIntyre, *After Virtue*, 189.

not readily understandable to those who are not engaged in the practice. Because of this, in MacIntyre's view it is those within—rather than those outside of—the practice who are qualified to critique it.[16] Second, as MacIntyre's definition of practices indicates, internal goods are "realized in the course of trying to achieve those standards of excellence which are appropriate to, and partially definitive of, that form of activity."[17] As one improves in a practice, the internal goods are realized to a fuller extent.

The internal goods are tied to the standards of excellence within a practice. When a person enters into a practice, she must willingly accept these standards. The novitiate must subject his actions to the judgment of these standards. Those who engage in a practice must accept their own shortcomings in relation to the standards. MacIntyre offers two examples of this:

> If, on starting to listen to music, I do not accept my own incapacity to judge correctly, I will never learn to hear, let alone to appreciate, Bartok's last quartets. If, on starting to play baseball, I do not accept that others know better than I when to throw a fast ball and when not, I will never learn to appreciate good pitching let alone to pitch.[18]

While these standards have an evaluative nature, the standards themselves are also subject to evaluation. They are subject to criticism and revision. But when we engage in a practice we must—at least initially—accept the authority of the standards as they are currently understood.[19]

One final difference between internal and external goods needs to be elucidated. Both are achieved through striving, but the nature of this striving differs. External goods are characteristically finite—the more I have, the less there is for others—so the competition for external goods results in winners and losers. Internal goods are achieved through striving to excel, but the goods are not limited. My enjoyment of fly fishing is not diminished if you seek to excel in this activity as well.

16. I agree with the general thrust of MacIntyre's assertion here, but I suggest that outsiders *do* have valid observations to contribute, even though they are not the ones who can ultimately identify and evaluate the internal goods.

17. MacIntyre, *After Virtue*, 187.

18. Ibid., 190.

19. Here MacIntyre makes a connection back into his main interest: the virtues. The virtues of justice, courage, and honesty are required to subject oneself to the standards of a practice. See Ibid., 191.

MacIntyre's Practices and the Christian Tradition

How might MacIntyre's work on practices fit into the Christian tradition? While the practices as set forth by MacIntyre are not specifically Christian, the overall thrust of his idea proves valuable in understanding the life of the church. I will now look at how this is so and I will point to ways in which his idea might be altered to be more adequate for use within the Christian tradition.

Craig Dykstra and Dorothy Bass are two of the writers who have taken up MacIntyre's idea of practices and modified it to refer to practices that are specifically Christian. By Christian practices they mean *"things Christian people do together over time to address fundamental human needs in response to and in the light of God's active presence for the life of the world."*[20] This definition has both its strengths and its weaknesses.

A strength is that Dykstra and Bass, building on MacIntyre, conceive of practices as traditioned and cooperative. They point out that this is significant theologically because it acknowledges God's decision to work in and through history in particular places and with communities of people.[21]

That they see practices as addressing fundamental human needs is an improvement over MacIntyre's definition. By their definition, an activity is a practice only if "it is a sustained, cooperative pattern of human activity that is big enough, rich enough, and complex enough to address some fundamental feature of human existence."[22] This characteristic significantly narrows down what may be considered a practice in the life of the church. These fundamental human needs or conditions include "embodiment, temporality, relationships, the use of language, and mortality."[23] Accordingly, chess, which MacIntyre describes as a practice, does not qualify as a *Christian* practice.

Dykstra and Bass extend MacIntyre's definition by tying Christian practices to the active presence of God. Christian practices are done in response to and in the light of God's active presence. It is God's presence that gives purpose and meaning to the practices and it is the Holy Spirit who shapes us into the image of Christ through our engagement with the

20. Dykstra and Bass, "A Theological Understanding," 18 (emphasis original).

21. Ibid., 26.

22. Ibid., 22.

23. Ibid.

practices. An awareness of God's presence and leading extends a practice by reshaping it and clarifying its standards of excellence.

Alas, my example of fly-fishing, while a practice in MacIntyrian terms, does not qualify as a *Christian* practice! Fly-fishing does not address fundamental human needs and it is not carried out in response to and in the light of God's active presence for the life of the world. One could argue that fly-fishing meets the need of relaxation or the need for a challenge, and one could argue that this practice is carried out in the light of God's presence which is so wondrously seen and felt in nature, but here we would be stretching the concept so far as to make it rather useless. Besides, while such demarcation between what is and what isn't a practice is helpful in a general way, this not the critical point of our discussion. The important thing is to both understand the general contours of the communal activities of the Christian faith that form us into the people of God and to *engage* in these practices, to *practice* them!

Dykstra and Bass would have a stronger definition if it lifted up the standards of excellence within practices.[24] These standards must be explicitly addressed because without them the practices have no positive formational norms. It is not enough for us to have a set of practices that shape us; we must have a set of Christian practices that shape us in Christlike ways, and this particularity is tied to the standards of excellence which for Christian practices include the rules, principles, and paradigms found in Scripture and the theological developments of the Christian tradition. Therefore, a practice within a church that forms nationalistic or materialistic people might rightly be called a practice, but it cannot be viewed as a good *Christian* practice because it must be judged deficient by the normative criteria of transnational Christian identity and freedom from materialism.

The definition of Christian practices set forth by Dykstra and Bass would also be strengthened by specific reference to internal goods. These goods are a key element of MacIntyre's conception and are necessary for understanding how Christian practices work in congregations. We can turn to Nancey Murphy to fill in what has been left out here regarding internal goods. Murphy, drawing on the work of James McClendon, dis-

---

24. Though they omit standards of excellence from their formal definition, in an earlier essay Dykstra and Bass do in fact discuss the standards of excellence possessed by a practice. See Dykstra and Bass, "Times of Yearning, Practices of Faith," 7–8.

cusses the internal goods of the practice of worship.[25] She points specifically to the pattern of God's initiative and human response that comprises worship. That God reaches out to us in worship is a good internal to the practice as is the joy and identity formation that come from responding communally to God in worship. We engage in worship because of the goods that are internal to the practice; we do not engage in worship for the sake of external goods. In fact, Murphy points out, Jesus specifically warned against seeking external goods from worship when he said, "do not be like the hypocrites; for they love to stand and pray in the synagogues and at the street corners, so that they may be seen by others. Truly I tell you, they have received their reward" (Matt. 6:5). Such status is a good external to worship.

Dykstra and Bass are right to point to the "responsive relationship of Christian practices to God."[26] This hints at the importance of internal goods. It is *within the practices themselves* that this relationship with God is shaped, experienced, and extended; the practices are not simply a means by which we prepare for a relationship with God that is then carried out somewhere else. For example, eschatology at first glance might be seen as connected to goods that are external to Christian practices, but as John Howard Yoder points out, practices themselves are eschatological because "the will of God for human socialness as a whole is prefigured by the shape to which the Body of Christ is called,"[27] or to put it another way, "the people of God is called to be today what the world is called to be ultimately."[28] Christian practices are not just a way to prepare for the fullness of God's kingdom and they are not just filler activities in which we engage while we await this kingdom. The kingdom of God is internal to the practices themselves. It is experienced and extended through Christian practices.

The idea of practices set forth here is based on the conviction that theory and action are mutually informing. As I stated in the above, I do not hold to the theory-to-practice model which sees theory as the place where values and beliefs are developed and practice as the place where these are then implemented. Rather, practices should be seen as theory-

25. Murphy, "Using Macintyre's Method," 34–35.
26. Dykstra and Bass, "A Theological Understanding," 21.
27. Yoder, *Body Politics*, ix.
28. Ibid.

laden. We may or may not be aware of the values embedded in a practice, but they are there nonetheless. Practices carry within them meanings and moral values. They are hermeneutics; they have embedded in them ways of interpreting. The beliefs conveyed by a practice shape the practitioners even if the practitioners cannot articulate these beliefs.[29] Practices foster beliefs and beliefs shape practices; a mutually informing relationship exists. And so Christian practices must not be viewed as simply a means of living out doctrines. Christian doctrines are indeed lived out through practices, but they are not external to the practices and normally emerge from practices.

MacIntyre's idea of social practices is valuable for understanding what goes on in the life of the church. Practices are grounded in tradition and are carried out by groups or communities, not by individuals isolated from other people and from the tradition. Practices are characterized by internal goods and these goods are subject to standards of excellence which reside in the practices themselves.

In addition to these characteristics, Christian practices are further defined by the fact that they address fundamental human needs and are tied to the active presence of God. To account for these refinements, I will be working with a modified version of MacIntyre's definition of practices, viewing them as

> any coherent and complex form of socially established coopera-
> tive human activity, *carried out with an attentiveness to the Spirit's*
> *presence and ongoing work*, through which goods internal to that
> form of activity are realized in the course of trying to achieve those
> standards of excellence which are appropriate to, and partially de-
> finitive of, that form of activity, with the result that . . . *communal*
> powers to achieve excellence, and . . . *the interpretive community's*

---

29. This is consistent with the approach to practical theology represented by Don Browning, among others. Browning argues that theology should arise from the life of the church and, after critical reflection, theology must return into the life of the church. See Browning. Craig Dykstra makes a similar argument in relation to theological educa-tion. He points out the inadequacy of viewing practice as "the application of theory to contemporary procedure." See Dykstra, "Reconceiving Practice in Theological Inquiry and Education," 163, passim. Miroslav Volf is a third writer who rejects the theory-to-practice model. He sees a reciprocal relationship in which beliefs shape practices and practices shape beliefs. Of note is his view that normally practices precede beliefs rather than the inverse. See Volf, "Theology for a Way of Life," 250–56.

conceptions of the ends and goods involved, are systematically extended.[30]

The fact that Christian practices address fundamental human needs is implicit in my understanding of the Spirit's work, and so I carry over Dykstra and Bass's meaning even though I don't carry forward their wording. Also, I shift from Dykstra and Bass's more general reference to God to a more specific reference to the Spirit. It is through the third person of the Trinity, the Holy Spirit, that God's divine presence and power are manifest in the world. I have changed MacIntyre's language of "human" power and "human" conceptions because "human" can be too easily understood individualistically. I have substituted corporate language for "human" in order to emphasize again that the practices are communal through and through, as an adequate ecclesiology must be. The ability of the community to achieve excellence is tied to the presence and ongoing work of the Spirit, which I inserted earlier in the definition. Human effort alone is not enough to fully realize the goods internal to Christian practices.

With this understanding in place, I shall now look at several Christian practices and note their intersection with our discussion of the priesthood of all believers.

SELECTED PRACTICES OF THE CHRISTIAN COMMUNITY

Reflection and evaluation of a practice are part of the practice itself. As MacIntyre has pointed out, the standards of excellence within a practice are open to evaluation and modification. He states,

> when a tradition is in good order it is always partially constituted by an argument about the goods the pursuit of which gives to that tradition its particular point and purpose. So when an organization—a university, say, or a farm, or a hospital—is the bearer of a tradition of practice or practices, its common life will be partly, but in a centrally important way, constituted by a continuous argument as to what a university is and ought to be or what good farming is or what good medicine is.[31]

---

30. My additions and substitutions are in italics. MacIntyre, *After Virtue*, 187.

31. Ibid., 222 (cf. 190). Nancey Murphy concurs: "such reflection is itself a part of the practice, the progressive refinement of Christians' concept of those standards of excellence that are partially definitive of this form of activity" (Murphy, "Using Macintyre's Method," 35).

Here I intend to engage in just this sort of evaluative reflection by seeking to identify and extend the standards of excellence of several practices that relate to the institution of the royal priesthood. I will discuss how the values of the priesthood of all believers are bound up within each practice and I will point to the standards of excellence found within these practices. My goal, in MacIntyrian terms, is to systematically extend the conceptions of the ends and goods involved and to further the ability of congregations to achieve these standards of excellence.

I have chosen five practices to explore in relation to the priesthood of all believers: witness, the Lord's Supper, discernment, friendship, and confession.[32] I have selected each practice because of its role—or potential role—in the embodiment of the royal priesthood in local congregations. Each of these practices, when done well, engages the whole people of God, not just some subset. Each of these practices helps to form a congregational identity that has the trinitarian marks of relationality, presence, equality, non-domination, unity, and differentiation.

Practices are multi-layered and so I do not intend to imply that the meanings I highlight are the only or even the most important meanings found in these practices, nor are these the only practices that carry such meanings. With these qualifications in mind, I believe that these practices are crucial in the life of the church and I believe that the priesthood of all believers will be more fully embodied as the church pursues the standards of excellence within these practices.

Witness

All Christian traditions agree that witness is a practice that is open to the whole people of God. When it comes to practices such as the Lord's

---

32. It is interesting to consider other lists of practices that have been set forth. Nancey Murphy lists five which she suggests are essential: works of mercy, witness, worship, discipling, and discernment (Murphy, "Using Macintyre's Method," 37). John Howard Yoder also lists five: binding and loosing (discernment), the breaking of bread together, baptism, the fullness of Christ (every-member giftedness), and the rule of Paul (participative decision-making). See Yoder, *Body Politics*. Twelve practices are found in Bass, ed., *Practicing Our Faith: A Way of Life for a Searching People*: honoring the body, hospitality, household economics, saying yes and saying no, keeping Sabbath, testimony, discernment, shaping communities, forgiveness, healing, dying well, and singing our lives. None of these writers claim that their lists are exhaustive. Also, these authors are looking at practices in relation to the overall life of the church, whereas I am focusing on a particular meaning as it runs through the practices.

supper or preaching, such consensus does not exist, but with witness we have a practice in which Catholics, Baptists, Lutherans, Pentecostals, and others can engage regardless of whether or not they hold office.

The practice of witness, which can also be described as proclaiming the gospel, is carried out through means such as evangelism, mission work, testimony, service, and godly living. In MacIntyre's terms, the practice of witness is coherent and complex. A group of Christian businessmen who are concerned about justice for their employees, high schoolers who go on a short-term mission trip, and moms and dads who teach vacation Bible school are all practitioners of witness. The range of activities included shows the complexity of the practice, and yet within this range commonalities exist that hold them together. One of these commonalities is that each activity is tied to the goal of proclaiming Christ crucified, risen, and reigning. Here we see how the goal of the practice is intrinsic to the practice. Treating employees justly is not simply a means to gain credibility in order to tell them about Jesus. Christ is proclaimed *in the act* of treating others justly. This activity proclaims that Jesus has ushered in a social order in which profit and power do not define human relationships.

Notice that each of these activities is cast in the context of the community. An individual parent must decide to teach vacation Bible school, and an individual teenager must decide to go on a mission trip, but the practice is still a cooperative effort. The gospel is proclaimed to the VBS children through a group of parents working together, and the high schooler is sent by a community and goes with others on the mission trip. This cooperative aspect is a point of connection for this practice with the priesthood of all believers. As people become more aware of how the practice of witness is a communal one, the practice becomes more participatory, and thus the people engaged with this practice live more fully as the royal priesthood. So witness contributes to the formation of a community that stands in contrast to the institution of individualism.

The practice of witness has internal goods. In general we do not pay people to witness. This would be attaching an external good to the practice. There are exceptions such as people who are full-time evangelists, been even here we insist that money should not be the motivating good. Rather, we expect people to witness for the sake of goods internal to the practice. One such good is the exercise of faith. Witness is a way in which faith is expressed and such expression is a good in itself. It is not tied to effectiveness or results. The missionary couple who labors in a hostile culture for decades without seeing anybody come to Christ can still be carrying out witness well. Regardless of the results, they can be said to be exercising their faith and such an exercise is a positive reward in itself. The internal good is not contingent upon positive outcomes. In contrast, in the institution of *technique*, positive outcomes (efficiency) are the good; this institution cannot conceive of an action that does not produce quantifiable results as good.

The practice of witness has standards of excellence, one of which is presence. James McClendon, who sees presence as a virtue essential to the practice of witness, describes it as "being one's self for someone else; it is refusing the temptation to withdraw mentally or emotionally; but it is also on occasion putting our own body's weight and warmth alongside the neighbor, the friend, the lover in need."[33] "Being one's self" is being authentic to who God has called a person or a congregation to be. But as part of the presence that McClendon refers to, being one's self is not done for the sake of personal growth or fulfillment but for the sake of someone else. In chapter three I suggested that presence is part of the nature of the Trinity. As people are present with one another, trinitarian correspondence exists.

When a person carries out witness in a way that keeps herself sealed off emotionally and mentally from the other, when witness is conceived of as a duty that does not need to involve relationship, then witness is done poorly. A man who speaks of Christ to his next-door neighbor in order to check it off the list of things that a good Christian should do is not being present with that neighbor. In contrast, consider a man who barbeques with his neighbor and knows the names of his neighbor's children and knows the things his neighbor's family likes to do. When his neighbor suffers a tragic loss, this man can be present with his neighbor and can speak of Christ to this neighbor in word and deed in a personally engaged way. Witness is done well when the practitioner opens herself up to the other, when the practice of witness is interactive, and when the practitioner willingly moves into the sufferings and joys of the other, as God moves into our joys and sufferings. Presence is a mark of witness done well.

Witness is done well when it provides a good picture of who God is and how God works. When we look back on the imperialism that often

33. McClendon, *Ethics*, 116.

accompanied the missionary surge of the nineteenth century, we judge the practice as deficient. We cringe at the fact that God was presented as an aging white male who wanted Africans to dress like Europeans.[34] Of course Christians argue today about what constitutes a good picture of God and we argue about how God works, but even so we have standards of excellence that are operative. For example, the Scriptures teach us that God is love, and so witness done well provides a picture of a loving God. Our picture of God must be much more detailed than this, but my point is that common areas of agreement concerning the practice of witness can be found among diverse groups of Christians.[35]

Witness done well invites people into the life of the Christian community. What is better: a Christian who lives out her faith in isolation, or a Christian who actively participates in her community? Would not the overwhelming majority of Christians agree that the latter is better? So, then, witness that invites people to a personal faith grounded in a community, rather than to an individualistic faith unconcerned with community, can be said to meet this standard of excellence.

The practice of witness builds up the priesthood of all believers in at least two ways. First, I have pointed out that witness is a cooperative activity, and therefore *groups* of people—*communities*—are called to witness. As Christians consider the standards of excellence in this practice, they should be moved to pursue witness as a group, and the practice of witnessing corporately will solidify their identity as the priesthood of all believers, a social entity that includes and binds together all Christians. Second, when done well, witness expands the priesthood of all believers. Others are invited, through the form of witness as well as through the proclamation, to join the royal priesthood. When an individual attempts to witness in a way that is devoid of communal content (e.g., a person who is not grounded in a congregation or a person who presents the gospel solely in terms of individual benefit), those to whom this individual witnesses are invited to join something that is not communal, that is not the church. Witness that is grounded in community invites others to join a *communal* entity.

34. These missionaries may have been living up to the standards of the practice in place at the time, but as I have said, practices and their standards are open to critique, and we should indeed critique imperialistic missionary efforts.

35. The creeds highlight more points of broad agreement that can serve as a basis for evaluating the excellence of a practice.

Preaching is a form of the practice of witness. In some traditions, this form of witness is reserved for ordained clergy. But like other forms of witness, preaching, too, should be an activity in which the whole people of God participates. What might this look like? Certainly preaching is participatory when those who are listening are led into the narratives of the sermon and are moved to respond in some way. Preaching in the African American tradition can readily be seen as participatory. But perhaps preaching should be participatory in another way as well: a variety of people in a church, not just the office holder(s), should be allowed to preach.[36] R. Paul Stevens describes how this works in his own congregation. The church staff is limited to preaching fifty percent of the time. The other fifty percent of the time, non-staff people from the congregation preach. Stevens points out that this arrangement allows for both continuity and room for non-office holders to preach.[37] Allowing non-office holders to preach is a powerful symbolic act. Visually, auditorially, and experientially a theology of the priesthood of all believers is enacted before the congregation.

In sum, the practice of witness is shaped by the theology of the priesthood of all believers and embodies this same priesthood. Witness is a communal activity and has a set of goods internal to it. The practice of witness also has within it standards of excellence by which the practice can be judged and extended. This practice, when done well, draws the whole range of Christians to participate in it.

While witness can justifiably be called a practice in its own right, witness can also be understood as the summing up of all the other Christian practices.[38] Every Christian practice, when carried out well, witnesses to the nature, presence and activity of God.

Lord's Supper

The Lord's Supper is a powerful practice of the Christian community.[39] Although this practice is interpreted differently in various parts of the

36. Leaders would need to prepare congregations for such a move by first engaging in interpretive and equipping practices.

37. Stevens, "Liberating the Leadership," 61.

38. For further discussion of witness as the canopy over the other Christian practices, see Barrett, "Embodying and Proclaiming the Gospel," 149–53.

39. I will use the terms "Lord's supper," "Eucharist," and "communion" interchange-

Christian family, some commonality exists regarding the nature and function of the practice in the life of the community.[40] The basic practice involves people eating a substance in the bread family, drinking a liquid derived from grapes, and making connections between this eating and drinking and Christ's life, death, resurrection, and his coming again. I will suggest ways in which the Lord's supper relates to our definitions of social practices and I will suggest some of the meanings in the Lord's supper that are related to the priesthood of all believers.

Here we have an activity that from its inception has been conceived of as cooperative. We participate in the Lord's supper *together*. Unity is an integral theme of this practice. The apostle Paul emphasizes the unifying nature of the Lord's supper when he speaks of sharing the cup and the bread and then says, "Because there is one bread, we who are many are one body, for we all partake of the one bread" (1 Cor 10:16–17). Recognizing the corporate nature of this practice is so important that Paul sharply warns, "all who eat and drink without discerning the body, eat and drink judgment against themselves" (1 Cor 11:29). He goes on to make it clear

---

ably. While several writers have set forth an understanding of the Eucharist as a practice, Miroslav Volf insists that sacraments be understood as different than practices. He acknowledges that one way of defining practices would include sacraments, but he states that a distinction is required because beliefs relate to sacraments differently than they do to practices: "core Christian beliefs are *by definition normatively inscribed in sacraments* but not in 'practices'" (Volf, "Theology for a Way of Life," 248). I am unclear on why Volf does not think that core Christian beliefs are inscribed in practices, unless he has in mind practices in general rather than Christian practices in particular. He seems to approve of the definition of Christian practices as set out by Dykstra and Bass (cf. Dykstra and Bass, "A Theological Understanding of Christian Practices," 18), but by their definition core Christian beliefs *are* inscribed in all Christian practices. I am not sure how practices—if they are Christian—could *not* be carriers of core Christian beliefs, and this is part of the reason I see no justification for distinguishing between sacraments and practices. Another part of my reason for rejecting this distinction is that I understand sacraments as those places "where human and divine activity coincide" (Yoder, *Body Politics*, 1). Thus I would push for a broader definition of sacraments than Volf is using, and such a definition allows for sacraments to be seen as practices.

40. Addressing the practice of the eucharist requires delicacy because of the strongly held differences regarding the nature of this practice. Is it a sacrament? An ordinance? If the former, consubstantiation or transubstantiation? I acknowledge the complexity of these discussions, but a detailed examination of these issues is not the purpose of this project. As I consider how this practice functions in congregational life, the theological contours I give to this practice will emerge. The explication of these contours in relation to the historical and systematic discussion of the Lord's supper is an important topic, but it is not one I can take up here.

that this body is the body of believers, the corporate entity we now call the church (1 Cor 12). As we participate in this practice, we are united with others in the body of Christ.

William Willimon points to studies in psychology and anthropology that support this idea that the Eucharist is a unifying practice. Psychological studies have shown that safe environments are most conducive to personality change and growth. Willimon suggests that the structured boundaries of the Lord's Supper provide this type of safe and supportive environment within which individual and group personalities can risk opening up to others.[41] From an anthropological perspective, says Willimon, communion can be called a rite of intensification, a ceremony through which a group "intensifies commitments to its particular set of meanings and values, and individuals become rehabituated to patterned behavior. A network of relationships is forged among participants and common loyalties are reinforced.[42]" The practice of the Lord's Supper is an action done *by* the community but at the same time it *creates* the community. It both symbolizes unity and actuates unity.

Unity is one of the standards for evaluating the practice: the Lord's Supper done well promotes unity while the Lord's Supper done poorly creates divisions. Paul rebukes the Corinthian church because some were being left out of the meal. The manner in which they were carrying out the practice was creating divisions, not community, and Paul upbraids them for this (1 Cor 11:17–22). Their practice was held up to a standard of excellence and thereby systematically extended.

The leveling effect of the Lord's Supper nurtures the development of the royal priesthood. The divisions to which Paul referred in 1 Cor 11 were divisions based on economics. The wealthy in the community were partaking of the Lord's Supper in a way that humiliated the poor in the community (1 Cor 11:21–22). In contrast, Luke describes a community that broke bread together and met the basic needs of its members (Acts 2:44–46; 4:34).[43] The table of the Lord is to be a place where all meet on equal footing regardless of economic status. The leveling effect of com-

---

41. Willimon, *Worship as Pastoral Care*, 174.

42. Ibid., 175.

43. In fact, John Howard Yoder contends, it was in part *through the sharing of bread itself* that the Acts community met the needs of individuals; it was more than symbolic. Yoder, *Body Politics*, 20–21.

munion is not limited to economics; the shared meal is a condemnation of all social stratification.[44]

The unity present in the Lord's Supper and the leveling effect of the Lord's Supper are both concrete ways in which the priesthood of all believers is manifest. In correspondence to the Trinity, the community of believers is to be characterized by unity. We are bound together through our perichoretic relationships with the Holy Spirit. The shape of our practices must be consistent with the unity of the triune God. Our shared life must reflect the Trinity. Paul's rejection of social stratification reinforces a mutuality in the people that reflects a mutuality in the Trinity. Economic power, social status, and rank of any sort must not be leveraged for privilege at the Lord's table, and because the Lord's table is a paradigm for the whole life of the Christian community and prefigures God's will for the whole of society, such levels of differentiation must be rejected more broadly as well. To the extent that the institution of globalization reduces this type of differentiation, it works in concert with the royal priesthood.

The manner in which the Eucharist is carried out should be consistent with these thrusts for unity and equalization. When a church invites ordinary people from the congregation to assist in serving communion, this is a powerful symbol of unity and equalization. It is becoming more common now for non-office holders to assist in this way across the spectrum of traditions. Let me push this one step further. While members of the congregation are welcomed to assist, can they themselves bless the bread and the wine? Can they themselves speak the words of institution? Indeed, unless non-office holders are able to participate in every aspect of the practice, the social stratification that is to be rejected by the practice remains.

As an example, I hold up the way the Lord's supper is celebrated in a congregation near where I live. When the Eucharist is celebrated in this congregation, four people are in front of the congregation: two pastors and two others from the congregation. As an expression of the equality and unity all have in Christ, it is always the non-office holders who say the words of institution. The pastors are certainly qualified to speak these words; however, though the pastors are key leaders in this congregation and they have gifts that allow them to serve in unique ways, they are not accorded a status different from the rest of the congregation, and this is

44. Yoder develops this point further. See Ibid., 22–25.

symbolized in the way the practice is carried out. This form of the practice builds on the ways the Lord's Supper has been practiced historically, but it also diverges from the most common historical patterns. At the same time, this pattern is embedded in the alternative historical narrative of the Anabaptist tradition with which this congregation identifies. This reflects MacIntyre's idea of a practice as both historically grounded and subject to modification.

The symbolism within the practice speaks to people regarding how they are to relate to one another and shapes them for living out God's desires for human socialness. Whatever approach a particular congregation uses, the symbols of that approach must work for, and not against, the unity and social leveling built into the Lord's Supper.

We have seen that globalization and *technique* can have a leveling effect, and where this is the case, these institutions can encourage the recognition and embodiment of this value in the practice of the Lord's Supper. The institution of individualism found in our culture is confronted and rejected by the practice of the Lord's Supper because the Lord's Supper roots Christians in the community of the faithful and invites the participants to communal unity.

These are not the only meanings within the Lord's Supper, nor are they the only ones that tie to the priesthood of all believers, but they serve as a starting point for understanding how the practice of the Lord's Supper is shaped by, and shapes, the priesthood of all believers.

Discernment

I have chosen to look at the practice of discernment because it provides a framework within which to consider the decision-making activities of a congregation, and the ways in which a congregation makes decisions provide one of the clearest means of seeing the contours of a congregation's theology of the priesthood of all believers.

So what should we do? This is perhaps the central congregational question for people formed by the cultural forces of efficiency and effectiveness. The rationalist mindset, which is perhaps as dominant in our churches as in our larger cultural context, will want to focus on efficient actions, and to be efficient, according to this way of thinking, we must delineate a streamlined process for making decisions so that we can get on with the actions. The decision-making process is put under a microscope for analysis and evaluation in order to help congregations make good and timely decisions. This approach is what John Howard Yoder calls "punctualism."[45] The focus is on the specific time, place, and circumstances related to a specific decision.

The Christian practice of discernment gathers decision-making into the broader effort to develop a sensitivity to the presence and work of the Holy Spirit. The practice of discernment does indeed include the operational and strategic decisions that a community makes, but it also includes an intentional, explicit openness to the Spirit that relates to the whole range of communal and personal choices as well as to an evaluation of authoritative claims set forth by individuals and institutions. Discernment is the practice that identifies false prophets as well as the practice used to decide whether or not to build a new church building.

When a small group or a congregation gathers to prayerfully talk through a situation, they are practicing discernment. It is a practice that encourages us to focus on the Spirit, not just on the decision. In discernment, as the community seeks clarity regarding a choice to be made, the community does so in a way that makes room for the Holy Spirit to lead and move within the process if the Spirit so chooses (and I suggest that the Spirit usually *does* so choose!). Discernment in a congregation is thus not very similar to decision-making in a business.

The difference between the practice of discernment and decision-making as understood in the business world can also be seen in the nature of the goods associated with the activity. In a business, decisions are made for the sake of external goods—primarily profit. But, as with all practices, the goods of discernment are primarily internal. I have already mentioned that discernment can be viewed as a form of witness. Here witness itself is an internal good. It is not the *goal* of discernment; it is internal to the process. Community formation is another good internal to the practice of discernment. The formation of community is not the goal of discernment or incidental to discernment; it is internal to it. The give and take of discussion, the listening required, the differences that must be worked through, the emotions that boil up at times—all these contribute to a sense of loyalty, trust, and cohesion among the participants; community both precedes and emerges from the practice of discernment.

45. Yoder, *The Priestly Kingdom*, 35.

I do not intend to gloss over the destructiveness and fragmentation that sometimes mark congregational discernment.[46] This sad reality does not take away from what has been said regarding the goods internal to the practice of discernment. By definition a practice contains within it different approximations of the ideal (if this were not the case, standards of excellence would be irrelevant). The standards of excellence within a practice serve as a means of critiquing these approximations. Not all instances of the practice of discernment will be carried out well, and in fact, sometimes the practice will be carried out quite poorly. But because practices have a historical dimension, a failure by an individual or community does not mean that the whole practice everywhere and always is corrupt.[47] Overall, discernment *does* witness positively to a watching world. In general, the practice of discernment *does* develop communal bonds.

We must remain aware of how discernment and decision-making are interrelated, but not identical. Because discernment is a practice, a punctualist view of decision-making is inadequate. Punctualism snatches a decision out of the narrative of the community, and discernment, as a practice, must be understood as an activity that takes place *within the flow of a tradition*. Discernment must be understood primarily in longitudinal rather than punctiliar terms.

This longitudinal dimension is important in at least two ways. First, the tradition teaches us about the processes of decision-making that have been used in the church over the centuries. As MacIntyre says, "to enter into a practice is to enter into a relationship not only with its contemporary practitioners, but also with those who have preceded us in the practice, particularly those whose achievements extended the reach of the practice to its present point."[48] We learn from the tradition which processes have been affirmed over time and which ones have been set aside.[49] Second,

46. Luke Timothy Johnson, an advocate of discernment, nonetheless devotes several pages to a discussion of the problems with discernment. See Johnson, *Scripture and Discernment*, 110–13.

47. This point is made well by Pauw, "Attending to the Gaps between Beliefs and Practices," 41.

48. MacIntyre, *After Virtue*, 194.

49. Nancey Murphy, in talking about communal discernment as a specific approach to decision-making, affirms this practice in part because the results of this practice have been validated historically. She states, "it is significant that communities that exercise communal judgment do not readily abandon the practice. This suggests that the results

our Christian tradition contains *other* practices that form us both prior to and during the decision-making process. Our decisions are not made in a vacuum, but come forth from our identities and values which have been formed over time prior to the moment when a decision is made.[50] Decision-making must be viewed as an ongoing activity that takes place within a larger narrative.[51] This confirms MacIntyre's definition of a practice as having a history, as being socially established.

What standards of excellence might be used to evaluate the practice of discernment? One standard is that of unity: discernment done well contributes to the trinitarian-shaped unity of the body. Unity does not mean that differences are ignored and unity does not mean unanimity of perspective. The type of unity that marks the priesthood of all believers and that marks good discernment allows for differences and distinctions—in fact, this type of unity *assumes* that differences will exist. As within the Trinity, unity amongst the people of God *requires* difference. If there is no difference, there is nothing to unite. This type of unity transcends differences without ignoring them. The Spirit indwells and unites believers who engage well in the practice of discernment even when they hold different views on a given issue.

Openness to the Spirit is another standard by which this practice is to be evaluated. Has the community been open to the guidance and work of the Holy Spirit in their practice of discernment? This criterion cannot be used as an exact tool, but it is still helpful for evaluation. If a group must admit that their awareness of and sensitivity to the Spirit's involvement in their process has been minimal, then their practice can be judged as deficient. Discernment done well is marked by honest openness to the Spirit.

A third standard for judging the excellence of the practice is one identified by Luke Timothy Johnson. He says that Paul repeatedly subor-

---

tend to be consistent over time since a practice that yielded erratic results would soon lose its appeal" (*Anglo-American Postmodernity*, 166).

50. Stanley Hauerwas makes this same argument in asserting that moral notions (he later substitutes virtues language here) precede decision-making. He argues that good decisions will naturally emerge from well-formed character. Although his argument has certain weaknesses—he relies too heavily on virtues as a means of achieving justice—I agree with his general thrust and find it helpful in thinking about Christian practices. See Hauerwas, *Vision and Virtue*, 14–20.

51. This is why I have placed decision-making in the midst of my discussion of other practices. It is one of many, neither the starting point nor the climax of the practices.

dinates individuals' behavior to the building up of community identity, and this, Johnson argues, provides a criterion for discernment: "the criterion is whether the interests of others as well as of the self are served."[52] Discernment done well is concerned for both the individual *and* the community, not just the former.[53]

What might the actual practice of discernment look like? Yoder, drawing specifically on 1 Cor. 14 and Acts 15, identifies a scriptural pattern of discernment that includes allowing all to speak, listening, and holding up the decision to be confirmed by the Holy Spirit.[54] By allowing everyone the opportunity to voice their thoughts and feelings on an issue, and by listening to each one who would speak, the community acknowledges that the Spirit moves in and through all the members of the community, not just certain ones.[55] The Christian tradition holds other related models; for example, that of Ignatian discernment and Quaker clearness committees.

Discernment must be seen as a communal activity, and as the community engages in this practice together, the ongoing process of weaving the communal tapestry continues. When communal discernment is done well, the voices of the lowly are heard and listened to along side the voices of the privileged. Outside voices are brought in, conversations with texts

52. Johnson, *Scripture and Discernment*, 119.

53. The list of standards for evaluating discernment can be extended by drawing on Nancey Murphy who sets forth two more standards for evaluating discernment: consistency and fruit. See Murphy, *Anglo-American Postmodernity*, 164.

54. Yoder, *Body Politics*, 61–70. For another discussion of specific ways discernment is practiced, see Morris and Olsen, *Discerning God's Will Together*, 65–93. Drawing on the history of the practice, Morris and Olsen identify ten movements in the discernment process and give significant discussion to each of them. A third move toward the concrete is that made by Nancy Bedford who, based on her experience in the church in Argentina, sets forth ten "moments" in the discernment process. See Bedford, "Little Moves against Destructiveness," 170–71.

55. I am making primary reference to communal discernment but I also acknowledge the validity of individual discernment. Frank Rogers is one who discusses both individual discernment and communal discernment. I suggest that what he describes as individual discernment remains a cooperative activity because the person practicing discernment does so having been shaped by the community, both historical and present, and, when "individual" discernment is done well, the practitioner will move back into community where this person and the community will live in light of the choices that have been made. See Rogers, "Discernment," 105–18. My view is in line with that of Morris and Olsen who state, "personal discernment is also vital, but it is always pursued in the context of community." See Morris and Olsen, *Discerning God's Will Together*, 64.

and context are included, and attention is given to biblical and personal narratives.

When done well, the practice of discernment is a concrete expression of a theology of the priesthood of all believers that corresponds to the trinitarian nature because it involves mutuality and participation. Such a theology of the priesthood of all believers elicits the practice of discernment in which the members *together* seek to speak and act in light of the presence and activity of the Holy Spirit.

Friendship

> I do not call you servants any longer . . . but I have called you friends. . . . (John 15:15)

In his words and in the way he lived, Jesus set forth a form of friendship that is paradigmatic for all human relationships. In this section I will describe how Christian friendships are grounded in the Trinity and then I will argue that friendship is an important Christian practice that draws people into the priesthood of the whole people of God.

Within the Trinity we see openness to the other without the giving up of identity. We see a relationality that is not just subsequent to personhood, but is definitive of it. And we see relationships that are marked by an equality that knows nothing of relational advantage stemming from power, position, or status. We see relationships that can be called friendships. Paul Wadell describes the trinitarian relationships in this way:

> In the divine friendship, the perfect outpouring of love between Father, Son, and Spirit results in unbroken oneness and a community that is never diminished by rivalry, jealousy, or selfishness. In God we see a community in which persons are not set over against each other, but a community in which friends flourish through freely given love. In God we do not find a community fractured through struggle, conflict, and domination; rather, we see a community in which differences of persons are celebrated, respected, and affirmed.[56]

These divine friendships within the Trinity inform us about how we are to practice our own friendships.

---

56. Wadell, *Becoming Friends*, 81.

The trinitarian model of friendship is further revealed in the coming, life, teachings, and death of Jesus. In the incarnation God entered into a friendship with humanity. Using the language of friendship to describe God's relationship with humans is a pattern grounded in the NT. God the Son rejected a relationship marked by domination and instead called his disciples his friends (John 15:15). In the end, Jesus demonstrated the highest level of friendship in his willingness to sacrifice his life for his friends (John 15:13).

The Trinity is not just a model, though. We also *participate* with the Trinity in friendship. Moltmann asserts that the Father's receptivity to our prayers is an expression of friendship—the Father's act of listening assures us of God's friendship.[57] We are also invited into friendship with Jesus (John 15:15). The root word for "friends" in John 15:15 is the same root for "love" found in John 5:20 where we read "the Father loves the Son. . . ."[58] The relationships between the Son and his disciples are not dissimilar from the love between the Father and the Son. These are all loving friendships. It is only through the Son that we can truly meet another in friendship. As Bonhoeffer puts it, "without Christ we would . . . not know our brother, nor could we come to him."[59] The third person of the Trinity is also necessary to our practice of friendship. The freedom and openness that mark the Spirit shape those who are open to the Spirit and in turn they become free and open in their friendships. It is the leading of the Spirit that moves one deeper into commitment and loyalty which results in a willingness to sacrifice for the sake of another. The practice of Christian friendships is modeled after *and* involves the Father, Son, and Holy Spirit.

If friendship is a practice, what are the goods internal to it? L. Gregory Jones describes three:

> First, because human beings only come to be fully persons in relationship, people need others to share goods, interests, and ends in a jointly pursued life. Second, friends are important in helping to provide the self-knowledge necessary for wise judgment. And third, intimate friendships extend and redefine the boundaries and conceptions of how we ought to live.[60]

57. Moltmann, *The Church in the Power of the Spirit*, 118–19.

58. This insight comes from Swinton, *From Bedlam to Shalom*, 80.

59. Bonhoeffer, *Life Together*, 12.

60. Jones, *Transformed Judgment*, 82.

These are goods that can only be obtained through the practice of friendship or a similar practice. They are also partly definitive of the practice itself.

The standards by which friendship can be evaluated include freedom, openness, sacrifice, commitment, and loyalty. These are "standards of excellence which are appropriate to, and partially definitive of, that form of activity."[61] These are characteristics of a good friendship. They provide an ideal for us to work toward in our friendships and thereby serve as tools for judging the inadequacy of our friendships. At the same time, they are partially definitive of our friendships—they must be present to at least some degree for a friendship to exist.

The practice of friendship develops a freedom that is to characterize the priesthood of all believers. It is a freedom to participate, to use one's gifts, to engage in the lives of others. No one can be coerced to participate in a friendship and no one can be coerced to participate in the priesthood of all believers. The sense of freedom that comes from the one builds up the sense of freedom in the other.

The priesthood of all believers, unlike other forms of priesthood, is marked by openness—an openness with trinitarian correspondence. This priesthood is not an exclusive social order. In fact, *every* believer is part of it, whether or not he/she acknowledges or acts on this. Practicing friendship well involves this same inclusive openness. As we learn to be open in our friendships, we move towards the eschatological maximum of openness that is to characterize not only interpersonal relationships, but also the structures within which these relationships are embedded.

What might this view of friendship as a Christian practice mean for church leadership? Christian leaders are to be models for others in the community (1 Tim 3), and so leaders must engage in the practice of friendship. Specifically, *pastors* must learn to be friends. Many pastors have been given the message that they must be careful to maintain a certain distance from their parishioners. They have been told that they need to find friendships *outside* their congregations because developing friendships *within* their congregations is considered too risky or is seen as leading to a diminishment of their authority. But the biblical narrative suggests otherwise. The God who chose to befriend us did not lose his authority by doing so. Entering into friendships does not diminish any

61. MacIntyre, *After Virtue*, 187.

form of authority that one has been granted by God.[62] Furthermore, the authority given by God to people is mediated through the community. It is not obtained or maintained by refraining from friendships, but rather, the authority appropriate within the church *arises out of relationships*.

I close by returning to the paradigmatic friendships of Jesus. He entered fully into friendship with his disciples. He openly expressed both his joys and his sorrows in their presence. He extended himself for them and asked them to do the same for him. He walked with them not just during the climactic moments, but during the mundane moments as well. He fished with them, he ate with them, he went hiking with them, and he worshipped with them. Jesus and his disciples were friends, and these friendships in no way compromised Jesus' mission. In fact, it was partly in and through these friendships that his mission was carried out. This paradigm calls all Christians—pastors and other leaders included—to enter into the practice of friendship. As communities practice friendship, they live out the inclusiveness that marks the royal priesthood.

Confession

Though it has taken various forms down through the centuries, confession has always been an important practice of the church.[63] I have chosen to look at the practice of confession because of its centrality to the priesthood of all believers as understood by Luther. Luther posited two main functions for the priesthood of all believers. One was to proclaim the word of God; the other was to *hear each other's confessions* and offer forgiveness, something he claimed every Christian has the authority to do.[64]

The practice of confession must be distinguished from the practice of forgiveness. The two are closely related but are distinct.[65] Both forgive-

---

62. Issues of confidentiality and appropriateness will arise in pastor-parishioner friendships, but these issues are native to *all* friendships. These issues are not unique to a pastor's friendships.

63. Thomas Oden shows this by weaving the writings of the Church Fathers and the Reformers into his discussion of confession (which is interspersed in his larger subject of communion discipline). See Oden, *Corrective Love*. Max Thurian gives a focused discussion of the Reformers' ideas on confession in the first chapter of his book on confession. See Thurian, *Confession*.

64. Althaus, *The Theology of Martin Luther*, 316–17.

65. Forgiveness has received much attention as a Christian practice, but to my knowl-

ness and confession can take place between a person and God, and both have a cooperative element to them. These practices are to take place not exclusively between God and a person, but are to involve other people as well. A difference between confession and forgiveness can be seen in their focus. With forgiveness, the focus is on releasing the wrongs of the other. With confession, the focus is on admitting the wrongs of the self. Forgiveness pushes for reconciliation. Confession pushes for humility and reform.

In the practice of confession, we acknowledge to God and to each other that we have fallen short of who we are called to be. We see here how the practice of confession relates to, and is necessary to, all the other practices. MacIntyre says, "to enter into a practice is to accept the authority of [its] standards and the inadequacy of my own performance as judged by them."[66] The practices assume the inadequacy of the practitioners and call for their ongoing growth and development. This comes about by the acknowledgement on the part of the practitioners that they have not lived up to the standards of excellence. To grow in competence in Christian practices requires one to admit the ways in which one falls short of the standards of excellence—to confess one's sins. The practice of confession is thus intertwined with all the other practices.

While confession needs to take place between an individual and God, it also needs to take place between people, and this latter interaction is my focus here. We can speak of two general categories of interpersonal confession: corporate and individual. Corporate confession is the most common form of confession in Protestant Christianity. It takes place in the congregational prayer of confession found in (some!) worship services. In this prayer, we make our confessions to God, but we simultaneously confess to one another. We admit to each other our sins of commission and omission. In this action we are bound together. Our prayers of confession establish our shared state of fallenness. We do not celebrate the fact that we have this fallenness in common, and yet the understanding that we *do*

---

edge no works yet have focused on confession in relation to a MacIntyrian conception of practices. My intention here is not to set forth a fully developed discussion of confession as a Christian practice, but to offer some of ideas that will be important in such a discussion. For the most focused discussion of forgiveness as a practice, see Jones, "Forgiveness." James McClendon shows how the practice of forgiveness is crucial for community formation in McClendon, *Ethics*, 222–31.

66. MacIntyre, *After Virtue*, 190.

have this in common can be a source of encouragement in our journey to move towards the standards of excellence in our Christian practices.

These corporate prayers of confession should be spoken by all those in the worship service, not just by those who are non-office holders. This cuts across the practice of some traditions, but it is necessary for the practice of confession and the priesthood of all believers to cohere. It is as we confess *together*, without special exceptions, that we most fully embody our shared identity as a royal priesthood. In the same way, the words of absolution should be offered in a way that does not stratify the whole people of God. A priest can do this by changing the tone and wording from "may the Lord grant *you* absolution" to "may the Lord grant *us* absolution." It can also be done by the whole people joining in pronouncing words of absolution to each other. The point is that the particular ways in which the practice is carried out must not subtly establish a special priesthood within the priesthood of all believers; the ways in which we carry out our practices are symbolically loaded, and we must work for the coincidence of our symbols—and the meanings embedded in them—with our stated theology.

How does individual confession differ from corporate confession and can it, like corporate confession, be viewed as a cooperative activity? Individual confession differs in at least two ways from corporate confession. In this form of the practice, it is a single person offering up a confession. The result is often an intensification of the experience as the individual must face the reality that these are *his* or *her* sins, not the often less pointed *our* sins. Individual confession also differs in that it is usually extemporaneous rather than scripted. This in no way reduces the value or power of corporate prayers that have been written on behalf of the congregation; it just points up a difference between the two forms. The extemporaneous nature of individual confession can focus the confession on the issues most pressing in an individual's life and can be helpful for expressing the particular manifestations of sin in that person's life.

Who is the person with the authority to hear another's confession? James implores, "confess your sins to one another" (James 5:16). We are to confess each other and we are to hear each other's confessions. Luther was right when he designated the hearing of confessions as a function for the whole people of God. It is not only office holders who are authorized to hear confessions. The *whole community* is authorized to do so. Some people, by virtue of their spiritual maturity and integrity, will be more equipped to handle the impact of confessions. Conversely, a person young in the faith may find the full force of honest confession to be a stumbling block. So practical moral wisdom will lead us to confess to some and not to others. But this discernment is not based on status or office. In principle, *any* believer can listen in this role.

While a sole person offers individual confession, it remains a cooperative activity because it requires someone else to *hear* the confession. The result is that we can no longer conceal our sinfulness from others. Such transparency allows us to break through to community. Dietrich Bonhoeffer emphasizes this point:

> Since the confession of sin is made in the presence of a Christian brother . . . he can confess his sins and in this very act find fellowship for the first time. The sin concealed separated him from fellowship, made all his apparent fellowship a sham; the sin confessed has helped him to find true fellowship with the brethren in Jesus Christ.[67]

As Bonhoeffer indicates, the practice of individual confession is relational because it involves a confessor and a listener and it is also relational because it moves the individual back into fellowship.

The practice of individual confession has a strong tradition in Catholicism where formalized structures and patterns have facilitated it. While these formalized structures and patterns have not been problem-free, Protestants have here a form worth emulating. What might it look like for Protestant congregations to set up regular times of confession? What if a congregation had people available during the hour before the worship service to hear confessions? What if regular participation in the practice of confession became an expectation of members, in the same way some churches expect members to be involved in small groups?

Indeed, the Wesleyan class meetings had such an expectation. As practiced in Wesley's day, these meetings differed from many small groups today in that these class meetings included a component of accountability. Confession is required for accountability to work to its full potential. Here the confession is before a group, not just before an individual. Wesley's class meetings provide another model for more fully engaging in the practice of confession.

---

67. Bonhoeffer, *Life Together,* 88. I wish to make explicit my assumption that this applies in every way to Christian sisters, as well.

As a practice, confession has internal goods. One such good is the lifting of guilt. We are promised that those who confess their sins will be forgiven and cleansed (1 John 1:9). Such forgiveness and cleansing cannot be purchased nor can it be obtained through means such as righteous living. It is a good internal to the practice of confession.[68] Reconciliation is another good internal to confession. True reconciliation emerges from the practice of confession; it cannot be attained without confession in some form. Not every confession results in reconciliation, but confession done well implicitly expresses a desire for reconciliation.

As with all practices, the practice of confession has standards of excellence appropriate to, and partially definitive of, this form of activity. Freedom is one such standard, a freedom that corresponds to the freedom in the Trinity. Confession done well must be done in freedom. Calvin stated, "confession . . . ought to be free so as not to be required of all, but to be commended only to those who know that they have need of it."[69] It is a practice that builds up the whole people of God, but only if people freely choose to engage in it. This freedom makes it more likely that true contrition will accompany the confession.

Honesty and true contrition are other standards of excellence for this practice. The more honest a person is in confession, the better this person carries out the practice. The admission of guilt, if not accompanied by a contrite heart, is a poor instance of the practice. While the practice of confession contains standards of excellence, these standards are used primarily by the confessor. Others often cannot tell whether I am being forthright or whether I am speaking with contrition. The standards can be set forth by others, and at times others can use the standards to encourage me to carry out the practice better, but because of the nature of this practice, I am often required to evaluate for myself the degree to which I am approximating the standards of excellence.

The practice of confession forms the whole people of God. It unites us in our sin and in our forgiveness. It confirms our identity as broken yet accepted. In corporate confession, we become aware of, and ask forgiveness for, the ways in which we as a community have fallen short. Our

68. Forgiveness can certainly be granted even when confession is not forthcoming, but it is still proper to speak of forgiveness as a good internal to confession because, though confession is not the *only* way to obtain forgiveness (it can be freely granted), we do not have a multiplicity of ways to attain it.

69. Calvin, *Institutes* 3.4.12.

commonality in the priesthood of all believers is brought to the fore. In individual confession I become transparent and vulnerable before another, *any* other from the community, and through this practice I am moved back into the life of the community, re-affirmed as a member of the royal priesthood.

LEADERSHIP, PRACTICES, AND THE ROYAL PRIESTHOOD

Christian practices are to be carried out by the whole community, but within the community, different people have different gifts and functions. For practices to be carried out well, one charism that must be exercised is the charism of leadership

Our churches would be in trouble without pastoral leadership, but not just any form of leadership will do. In this section I will describe a type of pastoral leadership that I see as being consistent with the nature of the Trinity and complementary to congregational engagement in Christian practices. My use of the phrase "pastoral leadership" should not be taken as referring only to the leadership provided by office holders in a congregation. I use it to describe the activity of any leader in the congregation, whether paid staff or not.

Mark Lau Branson sets forth three spheres of leadership that relate to the activity of a pastor: implemental, relational, and interpretive leadership.[70] In describing these three spheres, Branson notes that these are not three models of leadership; rather, these are three overlapping spheres of leadership that work together in congregational life.[71] A congregational leader will need to attend to all three layers at different times, sometimes separately and sometimes simultaneously.

---

70. His most focused treatment is found in Branson, "Forming God's People."

71. Ibid., 24 and 27. Scott Cormode offers a similar—though slightly different—paradigm in which he sets forth three models or styles of leadership: Builder, Shepherd, and Gardener. See Cormode, "Multi-Layered Leadership." He develops his approach from the work of Bolman and Deal who describe four frames for understanding organizations: the structural frame (similar to Branson's implemental leadership and Cormode's Builder model), the human relations frame (similar to Branson's relational leadership and Cormode's Shepherd model), the symbolic frame (similar to Branson's interpretive leadership and Cormode's Gardener model, and the political frame. For an overview, see Bolman and Deal, *Reframing Organizations,* 12–17. The rest of the book provides a detailed treatment of these frames.

Implemental leadership includes administrative and managerial tasks. The focus of this sphere is on organizing, structuring, and executing. Implemental leadership is required for budgets to be submitted, for programs to be given structure, for evaluation to take place, and for facilities to be kept up. Implemental leadership is concerned with organizational structure and execution. Without implemental leadership, the church would not do anything! When most people today think of leadership, what comes to mind falls into this sphere of implemental leadership. The institution of *technique* pushes us to focus on this sphere because implemental leadership is seen as the best means to attain efficiency, calculability, predictability, and control.[72] This is an important part of congregational leadership, but it must be kept in relation with the other two spheres of leadership and certainly must not be given priority over the other two spheres. In fact, given the nature of our current context, this sphere should perhaps be third on the priority list.

Branson's second sphere is relational leadership. This sphere seeks to build community and to foster healthy connections between people. In this sphere, congregational leaders act as shepherds who encourage, empower, and build trust in the community. The relational nature of the Trinity calls us to develop relational connections within our congregations, and relational leadership attends to this.[73] Leaders who do not attend to the relational sphere are wooden, dictatorial, or both! For our relationships to have trinitarian correspondence, they need to be intentionally cared for. The relational sphere must be present because "within congregations, families and friendship need leadership so that gospel meanings can be embedded and healthy relationships can be nurtured."[74]

This raises the questions of "what are gospel meanings?" and "how do we know whether or not they are embedded in our relationships?" The third sphere of leadership, interpretive leadership, is required for a community to address these questions. This is perhaps the most important yet

72. These are Ritzer's four characteristics of McDonaldization discussed above in chapter four.

73. In an interesting parallel from the business world, Charlotte Roberts also asserts that developing relational connectedness, or "intimacy" to use her term, is a key function of leadership. The motivation for Roberts's assertion differs, however, from the motivating factor in the church. Whereas the motivation in the church should be trinitarian correspondence, Roberts takes a functional position: intimate relationships result in greater efficiency. See Roberts, "Reinventing Relationships," 71.

74. Branson, "Forming God's People," 25.

least considered sphere of leadership. Interpretive leadership is required for congregations to engage well in Christian practices. Interpretive leadership helps a community to see connections between God, texts, context, congregations, and personal lives.[75] Interpretive leadership is about drawing out meanings from these connections. Interpretive leadership is about nurturing communities of interpreters.

This interpretive sphere can be further understood by looking at Scott Cormode's gardener model of pastoral leadership. The role of the gardener is to till the soil and cultivate the plants. The gardener creates the conditions for growth, but is keenly aware that she does not *cause* the growth. As Cormode describes it, "the Gardener plants vocabulary, sows stories, and cultivates theological categories that bear fruit when the congregation uses those words, stories, and categories to interpret their world."[76] The focus of the gardner is not on action, but on creating and pointing out meanings (which in turn inspire action). This can create discomfort for those leaders and followers who have traditionally viewed the role of a leader as being a "take-charge" kind of person. The gardener is not intent on boldly rushing forward. The gardener is intent on nurturing deep understandings that are not just intellectual or theoretical, but are also emotive and visceral in the way that good poetry captures the whole of our beings. Interpretive leadership is not all that our congregations need, but interpretive leadership is essential for Christian practices to function well in our congregations.

Alan Roxburgh suggests the image of leader as poet, which is another apt metaphor for this interpretive role.[77] The poet listens to the voices around her. The poet articulates what the people have been unable to say and the poet imagines what people have been unable to imagine. The poet's role is not that of strategist or manager; the poet is not concerned with functionality.[78] The poet asks challenging questions and invites a new way of seeing. The tools of the poet are metaphors and symbols. Roxburgh captures the poet's role well:

75. See Branson, "Forming Church, Forming Mission," 159–61. By texts he means Scripture, traditions, and formative stories handed down to us, both written and oral.

76. Cormode, "Multi-Layered Leadership," 90.

77. This image of leader as poet is one of four set forth by Alan Roxburgh. See *Crossing the Bridge*. He also describes these four images in his earlier work, *The Missionary Congregation, Leadership and Liminality*.

78. Roxburgh, *Crossing the Bridge*, 126, 131.

Functionality has become one of the mantras of our current ideology. Poets do not operate in this kind of world. Metaphors are not intended for functional purposes. They are meant to be lived in, savored, allowed to root down deep and take a form of their own. Metaphors are not to be controlled nor put to some practical use. They are like a virus in the body that surreptitiously enters the blood stream, lies deep in the body and begins a work of transformation. Poets use metaphor to create the imagination of an alternative world.[79]

It is the role of the poet to create new plausibility structures.[80] When people in the congregation are overwhelmed by the demands of their work, the poet imagines for them an alternative world where people work less hours and make less money but have more life. When an adult Sunday school class is engaged in heated discussions about politics, the poet helps them to see the structural powers and economic forces that are involved and to imagine how the texts of our faith might speak to this context. We need more than poets to lead our congregations, but we must have poets to lead us in the essential work of interpretation.

The work of the poet or gardener is not just to see *for* us, but to help *us* to see. As Cormode points out, the gardener's role is not just to interpret *for* the congregation, but to help the *congregation* to do interpretive work, to create *a congregation of interpreters*.[81] Interpretive leadership, then, is a shared activity, an activity of the priesthood of all believers. It may be the pastor who gives it the most sustained attention and effort, but the whole congregation must carry out the interpretive work. When a woman in the congregation who is considering a particular purchase considers the effects of sweatshop labor and how that connects with her faith commitments and purchasing choices, she has been formed into an interpreter. When a group from the congregation wrestles with how to connect their evangelistic impulses with the social needs of their neighborhood, we see a group of people who have become interpreters. Nurturing a community of interpreters is a long process—it requires the patience and faith of a Gardener.

79. Ibid., 132.

80. I draw the term "plausibility structure" from Berger and Luckmann, *The Social Construction of Reality*, 142–45.

81. Cormode, "Multi-Layered Leadership," 96–97. Branson discusses this same point, drawing on the language of the philosopher Charles Peirce who spoke of a "community of interpreters." See Branson, "Forming Church, Forming Mission," 158–59.

Empowerment of the whole people of God arises out of this interpretive sphere. Empowerment is often used to speak of something that is little more than delegation, and much of the literature on the empowerment of the laity falls into this category. But the type of empowerment I am referring to is *transformative* empowerment that emerges from the work of interpretation. A congregation needs to wrestle with meanings and needs to see meanings for itself rather than having these imposed upon it. Peter Senge argues that structural explanations (in our case, lifting up meanings) are *generative*, that is, they produce change.[82] While delegation produces a change in actions, interpretive leadership generates a change in constitution (which is accompanied by a change in actions). Interpretive leadership changes the way a congregation understands its identity, its place, and its role. It leads to internal rather than external commitment.

Chris Argyris describes external commitment as contractual compliance.[83] People functioning with external commitment carry out only what is expected of them or what they have been "contracted" to do. They do not define the situation and so they feel little ownership of it. In contrast, internal commitment is developed when people define their own tasks and when they decide for themselves the importance of a given task.[84] They develop a deeper sense of ownership in a project or organization and they are more willing to move beyond the initial tasks they have been given. Argyris argues that only internal commitment reinforces empowerment.[85] The internal commitment that emerges as a shared vision is not just an idea in people's heads but also a force in people's hearts.[86] Empowering the people of God is not primarily about allowing or encouraging believers to do certain things. It is about forming a people with eyes to see and ears to hear—faith attributes that, if real, will then emerge in good works (James 2:14–26). Empowerment is facilitated by interpretive leadership.

Cormode provides a helpful example of interpretive leadership. He constructs a scenario in which a local printing plant that is the primary

---

82. Senge, *The Fifth Discipline*, 53.

83. Argyris, "Empowerment: The Emperor's New Clothes," 99.

84. Ibid., 100.

85. Ibid., 99.

86. Senge, *The Fifth Discipline*, 206.

employer in town announces it is closing down. How might the pastor and the congregation respond?

> ... the pastor cannot change whether or not the Elizabeth plant closes. But she can highlight which portions of the plant closing story are most salient for her congregation. And she can select which stories from Scripture and from the congregation's history to place alongside the plant closure. This is how a leader working within the Gardener model makes meaning.[87]

This interpretive work sets the tone and focus for the congregation as it enters into the practice of discernment regarding how to respond to the news of the plant closure.

Interpretive leadership is exercised when a leader offers up the idea that one's daily work can be a form of witness. It is exercised when a leader invites the congregation to reflect on the connections between the discernment process in Acts 15 and the congregation's current crisis. It is exercised when a pastor chooses to confess his sins to another in the congregation, thereby setting forth a new (yet ancient) plausibility structure for how masters and servants, leaders and followers, pastors and parishioners might relate.

Interpretive leadership is exercised when, as a congregation prepares for communion, a leader speaks of the economic leveling symbolized in the bread and the wine of the Lord's table. It is exercised when the pastor explains to others why she embraces rather than refrains from friendships within the congregation, thereby helping others to imagine friendship in a new light. Interpretive leadership is exercised when a pastor points out connections and discontinuities between the priesthood of all believers, the role of the Holy Spirit, and the ways decisions are currently made in a congregation. It is exercised when a leader points out to a group that God is forming them in significant ways through their process of discernment concerning a specific issue. Interpretive leadership is exercised any time a poet lifts up the rich and formative metaphors and symbols of our practices. Interpretive work happens through vehicles such as Bible studies, discernment groups, informal conversations, Sunday school classes, and preaching. Interpretive leadership involves the on-going processes of articulating the meanings carried by our practices and challenging our practices when they communicate deficient meanings.

87. Cormode, "Multi-Layered Leadership," 96.

Our Christian practices communicate significant meanings and are formative; interpretive leadership helps to lift up and shape these meanings and seeks to facilitate formation that is consistent with our faith commitments. By interpreting the practices and by creating *communities* of interpreters, such leadership promotes the priesthood of all believers.

The goal of this chapter has been to mind the gap between theological reflection and the life of the local congregation. I suggest that Christian practices provide a way to close this gap. Our understanding of the priesthood of all believers can help us to carry out these practices well, and when these practices are carried out well, they have within them meanings that form and nurture the royal priesthood. Through interpretive leadership the community is helped to see and wrestle with the meanings embedded in these practices. In the process, the community is formed into the priesthood of all believers.

SIX

Conclusion

The royal priesthood is part of the essence of the church; it is not just a desirable feature of the church. For the church to live up to its God-given nature, the church must understand itself as a priesthood. All believers need to see themselves as part of this royal priesthood and they need to live accordingly.

I have argued that the biblical material not only opens up the possibility of the whole people of God being involved in the priestly work of the church, but actually makes such involvement normative. My claim is bolstered by our examination of the relationships between the Trinity and the church, and in particular, how the Holy Spirit shapes the church through the charisms. The institutions of postmodernity provide both opportunities and challenges for the priesthood of all believers. The church must interact with this culture, but the church must do so critically if it hopes to retain its unique identity as the royal priesthood, the body of Christ.

This identity can be lived out and extended by means of congregational practices. Congregational practices, when done well, form communities that understand themselves as ministering bodies, as priestly orders. Interpretive leadership contributes to the formation of such communities. These are communities in which all the members understand their callings to the diverse ministries that contribute to the in-breaking of God's kingdom.

In recent decades, a growing number of voices from diverse theological traditions have promoted the ministry of the whole people of God. I have sought to contribute to this upswell by strengthening its theological and ecclesiological underpinnings; I have sought to show *why* it is important for the church to live as the royal priesthood. By looking at institutions of postmodernity, I have also tried to bring an awareness to the discussion regarding the contextual challenges that the church faces in living as the royal priesthood. And finally, I have proposed that social practices are a concrete, communal approach for bringing these theological and cultural reflections to bear on local congregations. As the church more fully lives out its identity as the priesthood of all believers, it will more fully reflect the nature of God and will provide a more compelling alternative to the existing social orders.

SUMMARY OF IMPLICATIONS

If churches take this ecclesiology seriously, most will need to re-work their understandings of ministry. Ministry will come to be seen as activity carried out by any and all people in the body of Christ who seek to use their charisms to participate in God's work in the church and in the world. This is a view all churches would affirm theologically, but it is not a view embodied in many of our congregations.

Churches will continue to benefit from pastoral leadership, but as they develop a fuller understanding of the diverse giftings of the whole people of God, churches will not expect their pastors to be the primary ones engaged in ministry. Congregations will come to understand that ministry is shared among all the people. Pastors, too, will need an adjusted perspective. They will come to see the ministry of others in the congregation as of fully equal value as their own.

Pastors will make a significant part of their focus the task of interpretation. As pastors work with congregations to interpret texts and contexts, people will come to see how God is at work in their midst and how they are called to be part of that work—how they are called corporately to the priestly activity of ministering in God's name.

This ecclesiology has significant implications for theological education as well. Seminaries rightly expose their students to a range of subjects that are important for ministry, but they wrongly imply that students should become experts in all these subjects. This perpetuates the image of the pastor as omni-competent, and to imply this undercuts the priesthood of all believers. To support the ministry of the whole people of God, seminaries need to give more attention to developing the equipping and interpretive roles of pastors. Seminaries will also contribute to the priesthood of all believers to the extent that they take seriously their role in the character formation of the church's leaders, because humility and strength of ego are required for a pastor to give ministry opportunities to others without feeling threatened.

GOING FORWARD

The task undertaken in this project remains unfinished. In closing, I will outline six areas of importance for further research.

First, we need to do more work relating this understanding of the priesthood of all believers to specific denominational polities. Some church structures need to change, but I am convinced that many aspects of the royal priesthood can be better realized even within the framework of current polities. For example, Transfiguration Parish in Brooklyn, NY, operates within the official structures of the Roman Catholic church but functionally it draws lay leaders into a circle of leadership with their priest.[1] How might such patterns be extended within this and other denominations that have a hierarchically structured ecclesiology? How might such patterns be extended to churches that have little formal structure but functionally operate with authoritarian leadership?

Second, further research needs to be done to see how this theology of the priesthood of all believers relates to other cultural contexts. My backdrop in writing this dissertation has been the Anglo church in the United States. How might this theology of the royal priesthood relate to the Korean context or the Japanese context where patterns of respect and status are much more pronounced than in the Anglo US context? What challenges would this theology face in the African American context? How might the church in Eastern Europe take up this theology? At what points might this theology need to be modified to honor the values and patterns of other cultures and at what points might the cultural patterns need to be confronted?

Third, those who affirm my view of the royal priesthood need to continue in dialogue with those who hold a more traditional perspective of the priesthood and the laity. Because tradition carries forward—imperfectly—evidence of God's interaction with God's people in history, we

---

1. For a description of this congregation, see Barrett, ed., *Treasure in Clay Jars*, 143.

should not easily discard it. Yet, I suggest that while we should respect tradition and exercise caution when moving away from it, we are not statically bound by it. The tradition of the church is always open for examination and evaluation. If the church should change in the ways I have suggested, then further dialogue with the tradition(s) seems to me to be a necessary part of this project.

Fourth, I did not in a focused manner connect my conception of the royal priesthood to the current missional church conversations, but I think the two fit well together. The missional church is an identity of growing interest among ecclesiologists, missiologists, biblical scholars, practical theologians, pastors, and others. The topic of the royal priesthood has found its way into some of these conversations, but the role of the royal priesthood in the missional church project needs deeper and more focused attention.

Fifth, we need to give further consideration to congregational practices. I base my claims regarding practices on the work of Alasdair MacIntyre, but is his work supportable empirically? Do practices actually work in these ways in real congregations? How might we assess whether congregational practices really do bring to life the royal priesthood as I have claimed they do?

Finally, I would like to see more critical work done on the relationship between postmodernity and the shape of the church, work along the lines of what Michael Budde does in *The (Magic) Kingdom of God: Christianity and Global Culture Industries*, but focused on other parts of our culture. Other institutions of postmodernity might be identified and held up next to the nature of the church as I have done here. Additionally, other frameworks for understanding our culture can provide new understandings that might help the church to better understand its location in this culture as well as the possibilities and dangers posed by postmodern culture.

Because the priesthood of all believers is indeed part of the ecclesiality of the church, we need our theology, church structures, and practices to work in concert so that our congregations will live more fully as the royal priesthood. While in the present we work to live more fully as the priesthood of all believers, at the same time, we look forward to the day when the fullness of the kingdom of God will be upon us and the royal priesthood will be perfected.

Bibliography

Achtemeier, Paul J. *1 Peter: A Commentary on First Peter.* Hermeneia. Minneapolis: Fortress, 1996.

Ahlstrom, Sydney E. *A Religious History of the American People.* New Haven: Yale University Press, 1972.

Althaus, Paul. *The Theology of Martin Luther.* Philadelphia: Fortress, 1966.

Ammerman, Nancy. "Priests and Prophets." In *Proclaiming the Baptist Vision: The Priesthood of All Believers,* edited by Walter Shurden, 55–62. Macon, GA: Smyth & Helwys, 1993.

"*Apostolicam Actuositatem.*" In *Vatican Council II: The Conciliar and Post Conciliar Documents* 1, edited by Austin Flannery, 766–98. Northport, NY: Costello, 1996.

Argyris, Chris. "Empowerment: The Emperor's New Clothes." *Harvard Business Review* (May–June, 1998) 98–105.

Barnes, Barry. "Practice as Collective Action." In *The Practice Turn in Contemporary Theory,* edited by Theodore R. Schatzki, K. Knorr-Cetina, and Eike von Savigny, 17–28. New York: Routledge, 2001.

Barrett, C. K. *Church, Ministry, and Sacraments in the New Testament.* Grand Rapids, MI: Eerdmans, 1985.

Barrett, Lois. "Embodying and Proclaiming the Gospel." In *Treasure in Clay Jars: Patterns in Missional Faithfulness,* edited by Lois Barrett, 149–53. Grand Rapids, MI: Eerdmans, 2004.

———, editor. *Treasure in Clay Jars: Patterns in Missional Faithfulness.* Grand Rapids, MI: Eerdmans, 2004.

Bass, Dorothy, editor. *Practicing Our Faith: A Way of Life for a Searching People.* San Francisco: Jossey-Bass, 1997.

Basser, H.W. "Priests and Priesthood, Jewish." In *Dictionary of New Testament Background,* edited by Craig A. Evans and Stanley E. Porter, 824–27. Downers Grove, IL: InterVarsity, 2000.

Bauman, Zygmunt. *Liquid Modernity.* Malden, MA: Blackwell, 2000.

———. *The Individualized Society.* Malden, MA: Blackwell, 2001.

Bedford, Nancy E. "Little Moves against Destructiveness: Theology and the Practice of Discernment." In *Practicing Theology: Beliefs and Practices in Christian Life,* edited by Miroslav Volf and Dorothy Bass. Grand Rapids, MI: Eerdmans, 2002.

Bellah, Robert, Richard Madsen, William Sullivan, Ann Swidler, and Steven Tipton. *Habits of the Heart: Individualism and Commitment in American Life.* New York: Harper & Row, 1985.

———. *The Good Society*. New York: Knopf, 1991.

Bennett, David W. *Metaphors of Ministry: Biblical Images for Leaders and Followers*. 2nd ed. Grand Rapids, MI: Baker, 1993.

Berger, Peter L., and Thomas Luckmann. *The Social Construction of Reality: A Treatise in the Sociology of Knowledge*. Garden City, New York: Doubleday, 1966.

Boff, Leonardo. *Trinity and Society*. Maryknoll, NY: Orbis, 1988.

Bolman, Lee G., and Terrence E. Deal. *Reframing Organizations: Artistry, Choice, and Leadership*. 2nd ed. San Francisco: Jossey-Bass, 1997.

Bonhoeffer, Dietrich. *Life Together*. Translated by John W. Doberstein. London: SCM, 1954.

Branson, Mark Lau. "Forming Church, Forming Mission." *International Mission Review* 92 (April 2003) 153–68.

———. "Forming God's People." *Congregations* 29 (2003) 23–27.

Brown, Raymond Edward. *Priest and Bishop: Biblical Reflections*. New York: Paulist, 1970.

Browning, Don S. *A Fundamental Practical Theology: Descriptive and Strategic Proposals*. Minneapolis: Fortress, 1991.

Bruce, F. F. *The Epistle to the Hebrews*. Rev. ed. The New International Commentary on the New Testament. Grand Rapids, MI: Eerdmans, 1990.

Brunner, Emil. *The Misunderstanding of the Church*. Translated by Harold Knight. London: Lutterworth, 1952.

Budde, Michael L. *The (Magic) Kingdom of God: Christianity and Global Culture Industries*. Boulder, CO: Westview, 1997.

Calvin, John. *Calvin: Institutes of the Christian Religion*. Edited by John T. McNeill. Translated and indexed by Ford Lewis Battles. The Library of Christian Classics 20–21. Philadelphia: Westminster, 1960.

Campenhausen, Hans von. *Ecclesiastical Authority and Spiritual Power in the Church of the First Three Centuries*. Translated by J. A. Baker. Peabody, MA: Hendrickson, 1969.

Clarke, Andrew D. *Serve the Community of the Church: Christians as Leaders and Ministers*. Grand Rapids, MI: Eerdmans, 2000.

Coffey, David. "The Common and the Ordained Priesthood." *Theological Studies* 58 (1997) 209–236.

Congar, Yves. *Lay People in the Church: A Study for a Theology of the Laity*. Westminster, MD: Newman, 1957.

Cormode, Scott. "Multi-Layered Leadership: The Christian Leader as Builder, Shepherd, and Gardener." *Journal of Religious Leadership* 6.2 (2002) 69–104. Online: http://christianleaders.org/JRL/Fall2002/cormode.htm.

Dever, Mark. "The Priesthood of All Believers: Reconsidering Every-Member Ministry." In *The Compromised Church: The Present Evangelical Crisis*, edited by John H. Armstrong, 85–116. Wheaton, IL: Crossway, 1998.

Drilling, Peter. "Common and Ministerial Priesthood: *Lumen Gentium*, Article Ten." *Irish Theological Quarterly* 53.2 (1987) 81–99.

Dunn, James D. G. *Unity and Diversity in the New Testament: An Inquiry into the Character of Earliest Christianity*. 2nd ed. London: SCM, 1990.

———. *The Theology of Paul the Apostle*. Grand Rapids, MI: Eerdmans, 1998.

Dykstra, Craig. "Reconceiving Practice in Theological Inquiry and Education." In *Virtues and Practices in the Christian Tradition: Christian Ethics after Macintyre*, edited by Nancey C. Murphy, Brad J. Kallenberg, and Mark Thiessen Nation, 161–82. Harrisburg, PA: Trinity, 1997.

Dykstra, Craig, and Dorothy Bass. "Times of Yearning, Practices of Faith." In *Practicing Our Faith: A Way of Life for a Searching People*, edited by Dorothy Bass, 1–12. The Practices of Faith Series. San Francisco: Jossey-Bass, 1997.

———. "A Theological Understanding of Christian Practices." In *Practicing Theology: Beliefs and Practices in Christian Life*, edited by Miroslav Volf and Dorothy Bass, 13–32. Grand Rapids, MI: Eerdmans, 2002.

Eastwood, C. Cyril. *The Priesthood of All Believers: An Examination of the Doctrine from the Reformation to the Present Day*. Minneapolis: Augsburg, 1962.

Elliott, John H. "Elders as Leaders in 1 Peter and the Early Church." *Currents in Theology and Mission* 28 (2001) 549–59.

———. *1 Peter: A New Translation with Introduction and Commentary*. The Anchor Bible. New York: Doubleday, 2000.

Ellul, Jacques. *The Technological Society*. Translated by John Wilkinson. New York: Random House, 1964.

———. *The Technological System*. Translated by Joachim Neugroschel. New York: Continuum, 1980.

———. *The Technological Bluff*. Translated by Geoffrey W. Bromiley. Grand Rapids, MI: Eerdmans, 1990.

Faivre, Alexandre. *The Emergence of the Laity in the Early Church*. Translated by David Smith. New York: Paulist, 1990.

Fee, Gordon. *1 and 2 Timothy, Titus*. New International Biblical Commentary 13. Peabody, MA: Hendrickson, 1988.

———. *God's Empowering Presence: The Holy Spirit in the Letters of Paul*. Peabody, MA: Hendrickson, 1994.

Felton, Gayle Carlton. "A Royal Priesthood in a New Millennium: The Ministry of the Baptized." *Quarterly Review* 20 (2000) 369–82.

Ferguson, Everett. *The Church of Christ: A Biblical Ecclesiology for Today*. Grand Rapids, MI: Eerdmans, 1996.

Fiddes, Paul S. *Participating in God: A Pastoral Doctrine of the Trinity*. Louisville: Westminster John Knox, 2001.

Garijo-Guembe, Miguel María. *Communion of the Saints: Foundation, Nature, and Structure of the Church*. Collegeville, MN: Liturgical, 1994.

Gelpi, Donald L. *Committed Worship: A Sacramental Theology for Converting Christians*. Vol. 2. Collegeville, MN: Liturgical, 1993.

George, Timothy. *Theology of the Reformers*. Nashville: Broadman, 1988.

———. "The Priesthood of All Believers." In *The People of God: Essays on the Believers' Church*, edited by Paul Basden, David S. Dockery, and James Leo Garrett, 85–95. Nashville: Broadman, 1991.

Giddens, Anthony. *Runaway World: How Globalization Is Reshaping Our Lives*. New York: Routledge, 2003.

Gish, Arthur G. *Living in Christian Community*. Scottdale, PA: Herald, 1979.

Goudzwaard, Bob. *Globalization and the Kingdom of God*. Grand Rapids, MI: Baker, 2001.

Grenz, Stanley J. *Rediscovering the Triune God: The Trinity in Contemporary Theology*. Minneapolis: Fortress, 2003.

Hagner, Donald A. *Hebrews*. New International Biblical Commentary 14. Peabody, MA: Hendrickson, 1990.

Hansen, G. Walter. "Authority." In *Dictionary of the Later New Testament and Its Developments*, edited by Ralph P. Martin and Peter H. Davids, 105–10. Downers Grove, IL: InterVarsity, 1997.

Hauerwas, Stanley. *Vision and Virtue: Essays in Christian Ethical Reflection*. Notre Dame, IN: Fides, 1974.

Hays, Richard B. *The Moral Vision of the New Testament: Community, Cross, New Creation: A Contemporary Introduction to New Testament Ethics*. San Francisco: HarperSanFrancisco, 1996.

Hillyer, Norman. *1 and 2 Peter, Jude*. New International Biblical Commentary 16. Peabody, MA: Hendrickson, 1992.

Hobbs, Herschel H. *You Are Chosen: The Priesthood of All Believers*. San Francisco: Harper & Row, 1990.

John Paul II. *Post-Synodal Apostolic Exhortation of John Paul II The Lay Members of Christ's Faithful People Christifideles Laici: On the Vocation and the Mission of the Lay Faithful [in the Church] and in the World*. Boston: Pauline, 1989.

Johnson, Luke Timothy. *Scripture and Discernment: Decision-Making in the Church*. Nashville: Abingdon, 1996.

Jones, L. Gregory. *Transformed Judgment: Toward a Trinitarian Account of the Moral Life*. Notre Dame, IN: University of Notre Dame Press, 1990.

———. "Forgiveness." In *Practicing Our Faith: A Way of Life for a Searching People*, edited by Dorothy Bass, 133–147. San Francisco: Jossey-Bass, 1997.

Kärkkäinen, Veli-Matti. "The Calling of the Whole People of God into Ministry: The Spirit, Church and Laity." *Studia Theologica* 53 (1999) 144–62.

———. "Church as Charismatic Fellowship: Ecclesiological Reflections from the Pentecostal-Roman Catholic Dialogue." *Journal of Pentecostal Theology* 18 (2001) 100–121.

Kittel, Gerhard, and Gerhard Friedrich, editors. *Theological Dictionary of the New Testament*. Translated by Geoffrey W. Bromiley. 10 vols. Grand Rapids, MI: Eerdmans, 1964–1976.

Klaassen, Walter. *Anabaptism in Outline: Selected Primary Sources*. Scottdale, PA: Herald, 1981.

Korten, David C. *When Corporations Rule the World*. 2nd ed. San Francisco: Berrett-Koehler/Kumarian, 2001.

Kraemer, Hendrik. *A Theology of the Laity*. Philadelphia: Westminster, 1958.

Küng, Hans. *The Church*. New York: Sheed & Ward, 1967.

Lane, William L. *Hebrews 1–8*. Word Biblical Commentary 47. Dallas: Word, 1991.

Lawler, Michael G., and Thomas J. Shanahan. *Church: A Spirited Communion*. Theology and Life Series 40. Collegeville, MN: Liturgical, 1995.

Lösel, Steffen. "Guidance from the Gaps: The Holy Spirit, Ecclesial Authority, and the Principle of Juxtaposition." Paper presented at the annual meeting of the American Academy of Religion, San Antonio, TX, November 20–23, 2004.

"*Lumen Gentium*." In *Vatican Council II: The Conciliar and Post Conciliar Documents* 1, edited by Austin Flannery, 350–426. Northport, NY: Costello, 1996.

MacIntyre, Alasdair. *After Virtue: A Study in Moral Theory*. 2nd ed. Notre Dame, IN: University of Notre Dame Press, 1984.

Magnani, Giovanni. "Does the So-Called Theology of the Laity Possess a Theological Status?" In *Vatican II: Assessment and Perspectives: Twenty-Five Years After (1962–1987)*, edited by René Latourelle, 1:595–624. New York: Paulist, 1988.

Marney, Carlyle. *Priests to Each Other*. Greenville, SC: Smyth & Helwys, 1991.

McClendon, James William. *Ethics*. 2nd ed. Systematic Theology 1. Nashville: Abingdon, 2002.

McGreal, Wilfrid. "Developments since Vatican II: A Roman Catholic Perspective." In *Anyone for Ordination?: A Contribution to the Debate on Ordination*, edited by Paul Beasley-Murray, 112–23. Tunbridge Wells, UK: MARC, 1993.

Michaels, J. Ramsey. *1 Peter*. Word Biblical Themes. Dallas: Word, 1989.

"Ministry." In *Baptism, Eucharist, and Ministry*. Geneva: World Council of Churches, 1982.

Moltmann, Jürgen. *The Church in the Power of the Spirit: A Contribution to Messianic Ecclesiology*. Minneapolis: Fortress, 1993.

———. *The Trinity and the Kingdom: The Doctrine of God*. Minneapolis: Fortress, 1993.

Morris, Danny E., and Charles M. Olsen. *Discerning God's Will Together: A Spiritual Practice for the Church*. Nashville: Upper Room Books, 1997.

Mott, John Raleigh. *Liberating the Lay Forces of Christianity*. New York: Macmillan, 1932.

Murphy, Nancey C. *Anglo-American Postmodernity: Philosophical Perspectives on Science, Religion, and Ethics*. Boulder, CO: Westview, 1997.

———. "Using Macintyre's Method in Christian Ethics." In *Virtues and Practices in the Christian Tradition: Christian Ethics after Macintyre*, ed. Nancey C. Murphy, Brad J. Kallenberg and Mark Thiessen Nation. Harrisburg, PA: Trinity, 1997.

The Nature and Purpose of the Church: A Stage on the Way to a Common Statement. Faith and Order Paper 181. World Council of Churches, 1998. http://www.wcc-coe.org/wcc/what/faith/nature1.html.

Novak, Michael. *The Spirit of Democratic Capitalism*. New York: Simon & Schuster, 1982.

Oden, Thomas C. *Corrective Love: The Power of Communion Discipline*. St. Louis: CPH Concordia, 1995.

Ogden, Greg. *Unfinished Business: Returning the Ministry to the People of God*. Rev. ed. Grand Rapids, MI: Zondervan, 2003.

Olson, Roger E., and Christopher A. Hall. *The Trinity*. Grand Rapids, MI: Eerdmans, 2002.

Osborne, Kenan B. *Priesthood: A History of Ordained Ministry in the Roman Catholic Church*. New York: Paulist, 1989.

Pannenberg, Wolfhart. *Systematic Theology*. Vol. 1. Grand Rapids, MI: Eerdmans, 1991.

Pauw, Amy Plantinga. "Attending to the Gaps between Beliefs and Practices." In *Practicing Theology: Beliefs and Practices in Christian Life*, edited by Miroslav Volf and Dorothy C. Bass, 33–50. Grand Rapids, MI: Eerdmans, 2002.

Pellitero, Ramiro. "Congar's Developing Understanding of the Laity and Their Mission." *The Thomist* 65 (2001) 317–59.

Peters, Ted. *God as Trinity: Relationality and Temporality in Divine Life*. Louisville: Westminster John Knox, 1993.

"Presbyterorum Ordinis." In *Vatican Council II: The Conciliar and Post Conciliar Documents* 1, edited by Austin Flannery, 863–902. Northport, NY: Costello, 1996.

Putnam, Robert D. *Bowling Alone: The Collapse and Revival of American Community*. New York: Simon & Schuster, 2000.

Putnam, Robert D., and Lewis M. Feldstein. *Better Together: Restoring the American Community*. New York: Simon & Schuster, 2003.

Resolution on the Priesthood of the Believer. Southern Baptist Convention, 1988. http://www.sbc.net/resolutions/amResolution.asp?ID=872.

Ritzer, George. *The McDonaldization of Society*. Thousand Oaks, CA: Pine Forge, 2000.

Roberts, Charlotte. "Reinventing Relationships: Leverage for Dissolving Barriers to Collaboration." In *The Fifth Discipline Fieldbook: Strategies and Tools for Building a Learning Organization*, edited by Peter M. Senge, Art Kleiner, Charlotte Roberts, Richard B. Ross, and Bryan J. Smith. New York: Doubleday, 1994.

Robinson, John A. T. "Christianity's 'No' to Priesthood." In *The Christian Priesthood*, edited by Nicholas Lash and Joseph Rhymer, 3–14. Denville, NJ: Dimension, 1970.

Rogers, Frank. "Discernment." In *Practicing Our Faith: A Way of Life for a Searching People*, edited by Dorothy C. Bass, 105–18. San Francisco: Jossey-Bass, 1997.

Roxburgh, Alan J. *The Missionary Congregation, Leadership and Liminality*. Harrisburg, PA: Trinity, 1997.

———. *Crossing the Bridge: Church Leadership in a Time of Change*. Costa Mesa, CA: Percept, 2000.

Schatzki, Theodore R. "Introduction: Practice Theory." In *The Practice Turn in Contemporary Theory*, edited by Theodore R. Schatzki, Karin Knorr Cetina, and Eike Von Sauvigny, 1–14. London: Routledge, 2001.

Schatzmann, Siegfried. *A Pauline Theology of Charismata*. Peabody, MA: Hendrickson, 1987.

Schleiermacher, Friedrich. *Brief Outline on the Study of Theology*. Richmond, VA: John Knox, 1966.

Schweizer, Eduard. "The Priesthood of All Believers: 1 Peter 2:1–10." In *Worship, Theology and Ministry in the Early Church: Essays in Honor of Ralph P. Martin*, edited by Michael J. Wilkins and Terence Paige, 285–93. Journal for the Study of the New Testament, Supplement Series 87. Sheffield: JSOT Press, 1992.

Senge, Peter M. *The Fifth Discipline: The Art and Practice of the Learning Organization*. New York: Doubleday, 1990.

Shurden, Walter B. "Introduction." In *Proclaiming the Baptist Vision: The Priesthood of All Believers*, edited by Walter B. Shurden, 1–5 Macon, GA: Smyth & Helwys, 1993.

———. "The Priesthood of All Believers and Pastoral Authority." In *Proclaiming the Baptist Vision: The Priesthood of All Believers*, edited by Walter B. Shurden, 131–54. Macon, GA: Smyth & Helwys, 1993.

Snyder, Howard A. *Liberating the Church: The Ecology of Church and Kingdom*. Downers Grove, IL: InterVarsity, 1983.

Stevens, R. Paul. "Liberating the Leadership: Equipping the Saints for Full Partnership." DMin diss., Fuller Theological Seminary, 1987.

Stout, Jeffrey. *Ethics after Babel: The Languages of Morals and Their Discontents*. Boston: Beacon, 1988.

Stransky, Tom. "Congar, Yves." In *Dictionary of the Ecumenical Movement*, edited by Nicolas Lossky et al., 217–18. Grand Rapids, MI: Eerdmans, 1991.

Swinton, John. *From Bedlam to Shalom: Towards a Practical Theology of Human Nature, Interpersonal Relationships, and Mental Health Care*. New York: Peter Lang, 2000.

Thurian, Max. *Confession*. London: Mowbray, 1985.

———, editor. *Churches Respond to BEM*. Vol. II. Geneva: World Council of Churches, 1986.

———, editor. *Churches Respond to BEM*. Vol. VI. Geneva: World Council of Churches, 1986.

Tomkins, Oliver. "Mott, John R." In *Dictionary of the Ecumenical Movement*, edited by Nicolas Lossky et al., 703–5. Grand Rapids, MI: Eerdmans, 1991.

Trueblood, Elton. *Your Other Vocation*. New York: Harper, 1952.

———. *The Company of the Committed*. New York: Harper, 1961.

———. *The Incendiary Fellowship*. New York: Harper & Row, 1967.

Volf, Miroslav. *After Our Likeness: The Church as the Image of the Trinity*. Grand Rapids, MI: Eerdmans, 1998.

———. "'The Trinity Is Our Social Program': The Doctrine of the Trinity and the Shape of Social Engagement." *Modern Theology* 14 (1998) 403–23.

———. "Theology for a Way of Life." In *Practicing Theology: Beliefs and Practices in Christian Life*, edited by Miroslav Volf and Dorothy C. Bass, 245–63. Grand Rapids, MI: Eerdmans, 2002.

Wadell, Paul J. *Becoming Friends: Worship, Justice, and the Practice of Christian Friendship*. Grand Rapids, MI: Brazos, 2002.

Walzer, Michael. *Spheres of Justice: A Defense of Pluralism and Equality*. New York: Basic Books, 1983.

Warkentin, Marjorie. *Ordination: A Biblical-Historical View*. Grand Rapids, MI: Eerdmans, 1982.

Welch, Lawrence. "For the Church and within the Church: Priestly Representation." *Thomist* 65 (2001) 613–38.

Wiarda, Howard J. "Has the 'End of History' Arrived?: Globalization's Proponents and Opponents." In *Globalization: Universal Trends, Regional Implications*, edited by Howard J. Wiarda, 52–77. Boston: Northeastern University Press, 2007.

Willimon, William H. *Worship as Pastoral Care*. Nashville: Abingdon, 1979.

Wink, Walter. "The Kingdom: God's Domination-Free Order." In *Communion, Community, Commonweal: Readings for Spiritual Leadership*, edited by John S. Mogabgab, 157–65. Pathways in Spiritual Growth: Resources for Congregations and Leadership. Nashville: Upper Room, 1995.

Yoder, John Howard. *The Priestly Kingdom: Social Ethics as Gospel*. Notre Dame, IN: University of Notre Dame Press, 1984.

———. *The Fullness of Christ: Paul's Vision of Universal Ministry*. Elgin, IL: Brethren, 1987.

———. *Body Politics: Five Practices of the Christian Community before the Watching World*. Nashville: Discipleship Resources, 1992.

Zizioulas, John. *Being as Communion: Studies in Personhood and the Church*. Crestwood, NY: St. Vladimir's Seminary Press, 1985.